THE POLITICS OF
REDISTRIBUTING URBAN AID

THE POLITICS OF REDISTRIBUTING URBAN AID

Douglas J. Watson

John G. Heilman

Robert S. Montjoy

PRAEGER

Westport, Connecticut
London

Library of Congress Cataloging-in-Publication Data

Watson, Douglas J.
    The politics of redistributing urban aid / Douglas J. Watson, John
G. Heilman, and Robert S. Montjoy.
        p.   cm.
    Includes bibliographical references (p.   ) and index.
    ISBN 0-275-94716-5 (alk. paper)
    1. Urban Development Action Grant Program (U.S.) 2. Federal aid
to community development—United States. 3. Community development,
Urban—United States—Finance.   I. Heilman, John G.   II. Montjoy,
Robert S.   III. Title.
HN90.6.W38   1994
353.0081'8—dc20   93-25054

British Library Cataloguing in Publication Data is available.

Library of Congress Catalog Card Number: 93-25054
ISBN: 0-275-94716-5

First published in 1994

Praeger Publishers, 88 Post Road West, Westport, CT 06881
An imprint of Greenwood Publishing Group, Inc.

Printed in the United States of America

The paper used in this book complies with the
Permanent Paper Standard issued by the National
Information Standards Organization (Z39.48-1984).

10 9 8 7 6 5 4 3 2 1

Dedicated to our children
Shelby and Christian Watson
David and Catherine Heilman
Robert, Jr., and Clifford Montjoy

Contents

Tables / Figures

Table

Acknowledgments

The authors of *The Politics of Redistributing Urban Aid* are grateful to a number of people for their assistance in bringing this work to publication. The original research for this project was done to satisfy the requirements for the doctoral dissertation for the first author at Auburn University.

Several colleagues made important contributions to the development of the ideas contained in the dissertation and in the book manuscript. The second and third authors served respectively as dissertation adviser and committee member, and then as co-authors for the conversion to book manuscript. Professors Gerald Johnson of Auburn University and Thomas Vocino of Auburn University at Montgomery served as members of the dissertation committee and offered numerous valuable suggestions over the course of the dissertation work. We also want to acknowledge, with thanks, Virginia Prickett's dedicated, energetic, and efficient work on the typing and organization of the manuscript.

We are grateful to P. David Sowell of the Department of Housing and Urban Development for sharing his insight and knowledge of the Urban Development Action Grant program with us. He was also most helpful in directing us to sources of information that were crucial to the development of the dissertation and the book manuscript.

Finally, the first author is grateful to the City Council of the City of Auburn for its strong support during the writing of the dissertation and the book manuscript. The encouragement for personal growth and development of public managers by an elected board is unusual and is especially appreciated.

Douglas J. Watson
John G. Heilman
Robert S. Montjoy

1

Targeting Federal Aid to the Inner Cities

America's large cities are clearly in trouble. Serious urban social problems, such as broken families, drugs, and crime, are related directly to the cities' economic woes. High unemployment, serious underemployment, and failing infrastructures plague the nation's major urban centers. Unfortunately, the federal government has practically abandoned the nation's cities over the past twelve years. However, in the aftermath of the 1992 riots in Los Angeles and the election of a Democratic president, it appears likely that the nation's cities may once again receive attention from Washington.

Yet even if this national attention does come, it will do so in a time of declining public resources. The amount of money available for aid will be small at best, and the cities will have to compete with other claimants for it. This would seem to be a time for carefully crafted programs that leverage public money to stimulate private investment and that target public efforts very precisely to clearly defined needs. The concern of this book derives from experience indicating that there are powerful political* incentives working against highly targeted programs.

This book is concerned with the extent to which the federal government can effectively target its resources to the problem of urban America.

---

*The term "political," as used in this book, has multiple meanings, some of which refer to selfish or short-run motives and carry negative connotations. The term as used in this instance carries a positive and constitutional sense. It refers to proper self-interest of constituencies brought to bear on policy decisions through legislative, administrative, and other institutionally anchored processes of government.

Not all of the nation's urban areas are equally distressed economically nor do they suffer from the same level of deterioration of their infrastructures. In the past, federal efforts to target the cities with the most serious problems have not been especially successful; in some cases political factors have threatened the survival of these programs.

The last major federal urban program targeted to distressed cities was the Urban Development Action Grant (UDAG) program. It was enacted in 1977 as the cornerstone of President Jimmy Carter's urban policy. During the Reagan years, UDAG was continually criticized by the administration and its funding authorization was consistently reduced by Congress until 1989 when it was eliminated. This book examines UDAG as a targeted aid program in an effort to determine whether a federal program can be effectively directed to cities most in need. The dilemma that unfolds through this story is that the effective targeting and redistribution of resources undermine political support for the policies and programs that accomplish them. The political history, and demise, of the UDAG program has important lessons for federal policymakers in the 1990s as they struggle with how best to address the overwhelming crises in the nation's largest cities.

THE URBAN CRISIS

The problems of urban America have been well documented over the past two decades in the academic and popular literature. Jobs, like the white middle class, have left the inner cities for suburbia. The older central cities have lost large portions of their economic base yet have been left with social problems of seemingly insurmountable proportions.[1] The trend of locating private investment in the suburbs and in smaller, independent cities not only involves manufacturing facilities but also extends to office buildings and service industries.

Jerry A. Webman summarizes the trend:

> In brief, the transportation, infrastructure, density, and other advantages of the older cities no longer outweigh the advantages of other more dispersed places—the suburbs, rural areas, and newer cities in the South and West. No longer do manufacturers need to be near the railroads and waterways that brought them their raw materials and carried their goods to customers. No longer do most manufacturing firms find it economical to use multi-story factories to save on land costs.[2]

This "pattern of decline" has led to an erosion of population, jobs, and tax base, Webman concludes.

The plight of urban America over the past several decades can be seen in the statistics of per capita earnings of people living in urban areas versus those living in the immediate suburbs of the inner cities. In 1960, the per capita earnings of city dwellers were 105 percent of those in the suburbs. In 1970, the percentage dropped to roughly 95 percent and by 1987, it was 57 percent. Today, the percentage is probably below 55.[3] Evidently, the large cities are becoming the repositories of the nation's poorest citizens.

The 1980s were prosperous for the top 20 percent of the population in the United States. The income of the top one-fifth of the population grew by 27 percent during the 1980s while that of the lowest fifth grew by only 0.6 percent. Ironically, while the economy grew, the number of Americans in poverty increased as well. By 1990, over 33.5 million Americans were considered to be living in poverty.[4]

The Committee on Banking, Finance, and Urban Affairs of the House of Representatives reported on the effects of the "prosperity" of the 1980s:

- "Prosperity" meant more jobs, but also lower paying jobs: since 1988, the number of people working in the lower-wage service sector increased 13 percent, while the number of manufacturing jobs declined almost 6 percent.

- "Prosperity" meant an increase in the number of working poor: the number of *under*employed persons rose to 6.5 million; in Milwaukee alone, the number of working-poor families has grown 44 percent.

- "Prosperity" meant a startling rise in the number of persons unable to find decent housing at an affordable price: there are approximately one million people on public housing waiting lists in this country.

- "Prosperity" meant a decline in the homeownership rate due to an unstable work force, rising foreclosure rates, and a declining real estate market.

- "Prosperity" meant a rise in urban distress: crumbling and lost infrastructure, rising crime, inadequate education, and other social problems.[5]

In 1979, nearly 60 percent of the nation's poor lived in the central cities. Ten years later, the percentage had increased to 73 percent.[6] During the late 1980s and early 1990s, the abject poverty of the inner cities was effectively demonstrated to the rest of the nation through the problem of homeless Americans. From 1991 to 1992, there was a 14 percent increase in requests for shelter and an 18 percent increase in requests for emergency food assistance in thirty large cities surveyed by the United States Conference of Mayors(USCM). The USCM report urged the federal government to assist with the root causes of homelessness: unemployment, poverty, drug abuse, mental illness, and a lack of local resources to provide necessary services. One inner-city homeless shelter director stated, "There is a lack of affordable housing, a lack of job training and a lack of education. There is also the breakdown in the traditional family and alcohol and drug problems. . . . [W]e are seeing people from broken homes, dysfunctional homes."[7]

Not only are the nation's inner-city residents becoming poorer and more of them homeless, but the infrastructure that supports them is crumbling. Pat Choate and Susan Walter argue that the United States is seriously underinvesting in its infrastructure.[8] This underinvestment is most serious in the nation's older urban centers where "deteriorated public facilities threaten the continuation of basic community services such as fire protection, public transportation, water supplies, secure prisons and flood protection."[9] Public investment in infrastructure, including new housing, has decreased from 2.3 percent to 0.4 percent of the Gross National Product since 1969.[10] This trend of failure to invest in infrastructure is continuing despite overall increased government expenditures.

One of the principal reasons for inner cities' failure to invest in their crumbling infrastructure is the erosion of their tax bases. The largest cities are suffering to an even greater extent than the rest of the nation because of the long-term shifts now going on in the economy. Many of the nation's "sunset" industries are located in the nation's largest, most distressed cities. The House Committee on Banking, Finance, and Urban Affairs reported:

> The country is facing long term shifts in its economic base and industrial composition. As Professor Jon Goodman of the University of Southern California explained, "If you believe this is a recession, then you believe these jobs are coming back. If, in fact, you believe, as I do, that this is a fundamental restructuring of the economy, the problem with the loss of the jobs is they are not coming back." In reaction to current restructuring across America, our cities are confronting intensified distress.[11]

The result of business failures and relocations from the inner cities is a serious loss of their tax bases. For example, taxes from manufacturing paid 16 percent of Milwaukee's property taxes in 1972. Twenty years later, only 4 percent of that city's property taxes came from manufacturing.[12]

The federal government's role in aiding cities declined sharply during the Reagan-Bush years. In 1980, local governments derived approximately 18 percent of their revenue from federal programs. By 1992, the percentage had been reduced to six.[13] Funding for key urban programs was reduced by nearly 65 percent from Fiscal Year (FY) 1981 to FY 1993.[14] Senator Christopher Dodd told his Senate colleagues:

> Federal aid for employment programs declined from $8.4 billion in 1981 to $3.5 billion in 1990. That's in employment programs. . . . in Community Development Block Grants, we went from $3.8 billion in 1981 to $2.9 billion in 1990. . . . Mass transit funds were cut from $5.4 billion in 1981 to $2.9 billion in 1990. . . . And low-income housing programs were cut 80 percent in 10 years—80 percent in 10 years. That's incredible. . . . And what's stunning, I suppose, is people turn around and say, I wonder what happened. . . . What do you mean, you wonder what happened here when you've watched just an absolute abandonment and retreat from what's gone on in our urban areas.[15]

REDISTRIBUTING INCOME THROUGH FEDERAL AID

If the serious problems confronting the nation's distressed urban areas are to be addressed by the federal government in the 1990s, then programs involving the redistribution of income from wealthier jurisdictions to the distressed inner cities will have to be enacted by Congress. Redistributing wealth from prosperous areas to distressed ones involves numerous political obstacles. Those who argue for redistribution as a policy choice agree with Robert Stein and Keith Hamm:

> Cities with a disproportionately larger number of dependent persons, and which draw more heavily upon their limited resources to fulfill the service needs of their constituents, should receive a disproportionately larger aid allocation than their counterparts with a less dependent populace and a better-endowed tax base.[16]

Those who disagree with redistribution, or targeting of aid to distressed areas, argue that their tax money should benefit them directly and not be used to pay for someone else's problems. If federal aid is to be sent to distressed cities, Congress and the president will have to conclude that the failure of America's major urban areas is having an adverse impact on the nation as a whole.

The targeting of intergovernmental aid to distressed urban places is a fairly recent phenomenon. As late as the early 1960s, the federal government initiated targeted aid to depressed regions, such as Appalachia. In the late 1960s, assistance for the first time was targeted to the "urban ghetto." Under the activist leadership of President Lyndon Johnson, the number of categorical grants for state and local governments rose from 160 in 1962 to 379 in 1967. In 1965 and 1966 alone, 130 new programs appeared. Many of these programs, such as the Model Cities program enacted in 1966, were targeted to distressed cities.[17] Certainly, by the 1970s, the fiscal crisis in major cities, illustrated dramatically by the case of New York City, led federal policymakers to realize that the nation's urban areas were in need of directed financial assistance if they were to survive.[18]

Despite this realization, President Richard Nixon's "New Federalism" proposals involved consolidation of many categorical programs with narrow purposes to broader, more flexible block grants. Community Development Block Grants, General Revenue Sharing, the Comprehensive Employment Training Act (CETA) grants, and three other block grant programs replaced numerous categorical grants.[19] The block grant programs tended to be more distributive and less targeted to the most needy cities.

THE UDAG EXPERIENCE

In the late 1970s, the Carter administration proposed, and Congress approved, the Urban Development Action Grant (UDAG)** program. In contrast to the block grant approach, it was designed to target economic development aid to distressed cities. One at least implicit purpose of a targeted economic development program, such as UDAG, is to achieve "geographic income redistribution, or at least a slowing down of market forces to prevent a continuing redistribution away from distressed places."[20]

The legislation authorizing UDAG directed the Department of Housing and Urban Development (HUD) to use the funds in "severely distressed cities and urban counties to help alleviate physical and economic deterioration."[21] Official indicators of deterioration included excessive abandonment by the white middle class, dilapidated housing, population loss, or declining tax base.

As HUD later reported, the symptoms of distress identified in the legislation were commonplace in America's urban places of the mid-1970s: declining employment opportunities, fiscal strain, residential abandonment due to white flight to suburbia, high unemployment, poverty, aging infrastructure, and obsolete land use patterns.[22] The UDAG program was aimed at attacking these problems by providing

---

**Note:* The term UDAG is used as both a noun and an adjective. As a noun, UDAG can refer to either the federal program or to a specific grant made to a locality under the program. As an adjective, UDAG can modify either individual grants or the entire program. In both cases, context will indicate which meaning is intended.

financing to stimulate private investment that otherwise would not be made in distressed communities.

UDAG differed from prior federal economic development programs because of its emphasis on public-private partnerships. Local governments were required to negotiate with the private sector for firm financial commitments before applying for UDAG assistance. The UDAG supplemental assistance was to be used to provide necessary infrastructure or to bridge financing gaps that prevented projects from otherwise going forward. UDAGs were to be approved only for development projects that were privately sponsored, financed, and managed and that contributed to community development goals of job creation, improved housing, and strengthened tax base.[23] An additional condition was that the local governments be able to certify that "but for" the UDAG financing, the proposed project would not go forward.

Over the life of the UDAG program, Congress appropriated $4.6 billion to be used for projects in one of three categories—industrial, commercial, or housing (neighborhood). One-fourth of the funds were set aside for small cities, which competed for funding separately from large cities. At the end of the program, HUD claimed that nearly $32 billion of private funds and over $1.9 billion in other public funds had been invested in its UDAG projects. Commercial projects received half of the UDAG funds: industrial projects, 24 percent; housing projects, 11 percent; and mixed projects, 15 percent. Nearly two-thirds of the funds granted to local governments were used as loans to developers and cities can retain these funds as the loans are paid back. As a result, local governments should receive nearly $1 billion in loan paybacks by the mid-1990s. It is noteworthy that cities will have the capacity to continue to create economic development through the next decade and beyond with repaid UDAG funds, if they so choose.

In sum, in very general terms the UDAG policy did what it was supposed to do: it targeted resources to local governments that needed help to achieve economic development. Given the continuing problems of urban America, and in the first year of a new presidential administration, explanations for the death of UDAG are of immediate interest.

This book will develop and test the view that programs of economic redistribution contain the political seeds of their own demise. The book will show that UDAG died because of political controversy generated by its partly apparent and partly real success in targeting funds to cities in need. Its downfall resulted in large part from its having done what it was intended to do. UDAG redistributed wealth among government entities by allocating federal tax revenue to selected local governments.

Several aspects of the UDAG program created continuing political problems.[24] First, since UDAG was aimed specifically at distressed cities, the notion of "distress" needed to be defined. Congress gave HUD responsibility for developing the formula for "distress" and, thereby, determining which cities were eligible for funding. Under the formula developed by HUD, older large cities and urban counties in the Northeast and Midwest were more heavily distressed, so a higher percentage of the funding went to them.[25] This result appears to have caused a lessening of political support for the program among local leaders and members of Congress from the South and West.

Second, UDAGs were not to be granted by HUD unless there was a valid "but for" clause, which stated that the project would not be developed except for the presence of the UDAG.[26] Early studies by the General Accounting Office (GAO) and by HUD indicated that a number of funded projects would have been built regardless of the UDAG funding. These charges clouded HUD's claims that UDAG had created nearly $32 billion of private investment and 589,800 new permanent jobs for the $4.6 billion UDAG funding.[27] A possible consequence was further decline in political support for the UDAG program.

Third, UDAGs were awarded to local governments that, in turn, provided the money to private developers in the form of loans, grants, or both. As the program matured, HUD encouraged cities to lend the money, recapture the funds through paybacks, and establish revolving loan funds to make further loans for other projects. Of the $4.6 billion appropriated by Congress, $2.9 billion was used for loans to developers. Through FY 1988, over $455 million had been paid back to cities, and as of FY 1993, nearly $1 billion was to have been repaid.[28] Some cities did create sound loan programs emphasizing job creation for low- and moderate-income citizens.[29] Political problems arose, however, because other cities elected to forgive the original loans, and still others used repaid loan receipts to finance high-risk ventures. David Rymph and Jack Underhill report that 9.3 percent of the developers of UDAG projects nationally have declared bankruptcy.[30] This high bankruptcy rate raised questions about the financial soundness of many of the UDAG projects.

Fourth, following the termination of UDAG, Congress investigated wrongdoing in the Department of Housing and Urban Development (HUD) and discovered that the secretary of HUD had manipulated the UDAG funding system for political purposes. Testimony before Congress described how the political appointees in the Department, including the secretary and a few close aides, came into conflict with career employees over their efforts to politicize the UDAG process. The career staff was dedicated to the principles of targeting UDAG to the nation's most distressed cities regardless of political influence. In this regard, UDAG provides a vivid example of how a targeted program can be undermined by political interference.

Throughout its history the UDAG program faced a number of serious political problems. However, it also pioneered several important changes in the relationships between public (especially local) and private organizations. For example, prior to UDAG, cities generally did not play a proactive role in development financing. With UDAG, cities sought investors with the enticement of equity participation by the local governments. Local governments, for the first time in the modern era, became entrepreneurs in traditionally private sector ventures as investment partners.[31]

IMPLICATIONS FOR URBAN POLICY

The UDAG program contains several important lessons for urban policymakers in the 1990s. First, UDAG demonstrated that the private sector can be enticed to participate with the public sector in urban development activities. This conclusion is important here because any new program must involve private sector investment if the economic troubles of the cities are to be addressed.

The issue of how to structure effective public-private arrangements for urban development is far from resolved. At present, two interesting experiments are under way utilizing private sector approaches to address urban ills in Atlanta and Los Angeles. If these experiments in addressing the crises in the inner cities of these two major metropolitan areas are successful, it is likely they will be duplicated across the country and become models for the latter 1990s.

In Atlanta, former President Jimmy Carter founded the Atlanta Project, which has targeted that city's twenty most distressed neighborhoods. Over $22 million has been donated for the Atlanta Project and over 110,000 volunteers have offered their services. In Los Angeles, Peter Ueberroth, who chaired the 1984 Olympics there, headed Rebuild Los Angeles (RLA), a massive effort to lure corporations to locate in the poorest sections of the inner city. RLA's goal is to create 60,000 new permanent jobs in the target area over its first five years.[32]

The Atlanta and Los Angeles efforts share several fundamental similarities: (1) their initiative, leadership, philosophy, and most of their resources are derived from the private sector; (2) they depend on the involvement and commitment of the inner city residents to make decisions on the direction their programs will take; (3) they are approaching the problems in their communities in a comprehensive way. For example, the Atlanta Project hopes to eliminate "a laundry list of the city's most distressing ills, including hunger, joblessness, drug addiction, homelessness and violence."[33]

Following the Los Angeles riots, Congress enacted a $1 billion emergency program to provide summer jobs for central city youths, as well as aid for businesses and residents of Los Angeles and Chicago. In July 1992, President Bush and congressional leaders apparently agreed on an urban aid plan for a limited number of distressed cities. Under the agreement, fifty enterprise zones were to be established in twenty-five distressed urban areas and twenty-five distressed rural areas. While $2.5 billion was allocated for social and law enforcement programs in the zones, the primary emphasis of the legislation was on attracting new businesses through generous federal tax breaks. The twenty-five urban enterprise zones were to be selected by the Department of Housing and Urban Development from neighborhoods with unemployment rates at least one and one-half times greater than the national average and with more than 20 percent of the residents living in poverty.[34] Despite strong pressure from over 200 public and private organizations to sign the bill into law, President Bush vetoed it in the late fall of 1992.[35]

A second lesson learned from the UDAG experience has to do with a theoretical question that derives from the influential work of Theodore Lowi. The question is whether our political system has built into it structural limits that will make redistributive programs fail. We know that pressure to convert redistributive programs to distributive ones (programs that allocate resources relatively evenly) comes from representatives of jurisdictions that are not benefiting from the programs. The question is whether these forces are so powerfully at work in our political system as to foredoom redistributive programs aimed at the urban crisis.

An illustration of this pressure toward distributive programs was reported by the *New York Times* at the time of passage by the House of Representatives of the July 1992 urban aid bill:

> To garner the votes of rural lawmakers, 25 more enterprise zones will be selected in impoverished farming areas, and they will receive about 20 percent, or $1 billion, of the tax and program benefits. "Anyone who calls this 'urban aid' can't read," said Representative Charles B. Rangel, Democrat of Harlem, who voted for the bill.[36]

A third lesson of UDAG is that there must be agreement on the definition of what constitutes a distressed city. Preferably, agreement should be reached by Congress and the president and reflected in the enabling legislation. Political pressures to broaden the definition to be more inclusive are very strong. That those pressures will be exerted in Congress, just as they would be on Department of Housing and Urban Development officials, is certain. However, as long as Congress is committed to the concept of targeting aid because it is in the nation's overall interest, it will be in a better position to reinforce the redistributive concept of a new urban program.

THE REMAINING CHAPTERS

Chapter 2 provides the theoretical support for the analysis developed in Chapters 3, 4, and 5. It reviews what other authors have written about topics including the effectiveness of targeting of intergovernmental aid, Theodore Lowi's theory of policy types, and empirical studies on UDAG's targeting effectiveness. Chapter 2 also brings into focus the question of whether program administrators could respond effectively to political pressures on redistributive programs if they had sufficient discretion in program implementation.

Chapter 3 reviews the political history of the UDAG program from its introduction to its demise. Emphasis is placed on events, developments, and actions that were related to targeting, such as the broadening of the program to increase constituency and congressional support.

Chapter 4 examines three major issues in targeting as found in studies completed on UDAG by HUD and GAO. The studies are important not only for their findings but because they reflected congressional concern over questions of targeting.

Chapter 5 analyzes the quantitative data on UDAG to determine how effectively UDAG was targeted to the nation's most distressed cities. Chapter 6 presents findings and conclusions, and suggests broader implications of the study for the concept of targeting and the theory of policy types.

NOTES

1. Kirk Johnson, "Take Our Poor, Angry Hartford Tells Suburbs," *New York Times*, 11 February 1991, A1 and A13.

2. Jerry A. Webman, "UDAG: Targeting Urban Economic Development," *Political Science Quarterly* 96-2 (Summer 1981): 194.

3. Congress, Senate, Committee on Banking, Housing, and Urban Affairs, *The Economic Condition of Our Nation's Cities*, 102nd Cong., 2nd Sess., 30 January 1992, 10.

4. Congress, House, Committee on Banking, Finance, and Urban Affairs, *Economic Distress in Our Cities*, 102nd Cong., 2nd Sess., April 1992, 4.

5. Ibid., 1.

6. Ibid., 8.

7. Karin Meadows, "Homeless Find Room in Inn, Shelters Boast," *The Birmingham News–Birmingham Post Herald*, 12 December 1992, 1A and 14A.

8. Pat Choate and Susan Walter, *America in Ruins—Beyond the Public Works Pork Barrel* (Washington, D.C.: Council of State Planning Agencies, 1981), 1.

9. Ibid.

10. Congress, House, Committee on Banking, Finance, and Urban Affairs, *Economic Distress in Our Cities*, 102nd Cong., 2nd Sess., April 1992, 5.

11. Ibid., 7.

12. Ibid., 8.

13. Congress, Senate, Committee on Banking, Housing, and Urban Affairs, *The Economic Condition of Our Nation's Cities*, 102nd Cong., 2nd Sess., 30 January 1992, 10.

14. Ibid., 59.

15. Ibid., 10–11.

16. Robert M. Stein and Keith E. Hamm, "A Comparative Analysis of Targeting Capacity of State and Federal Intergovernmental Aid Allocations: 1977, 1982," *Social Sciences Quarterly* 68 (September 1987): 449.

17. George E. Hale and Marian Lief Palley, *The Politics of Federal Grants* (Washington, D.C.: Congressional Quarterly Press, 1981), 12–17.

18. Susan S. Jacobs and Elizabeth A. Roistacher, "The Urban Impacts of HUD's Urban Development Action Grant Program, or, Where's the Action in Action Grants?" in *The Urban Impacts of Federal Policies*, ed. Norman J. Glickman (Baltimore: Johns Hopkins University Press, 1980), 337.

19. Hale and Palley, 110.

20. Jacobs and Roistacher, 337.

21. Department of Housing and Urban Development, Office of Community Planning and Development, *Urban Development Action Grant Program— Second Annual Report* (Washington, D.C.: U.S. Department of Housing and Urban Development, 1980), 1.

22. Ibid.

23. Ibid.

24. Ingrid W. Reed, "Life and Death of UDAG: An Assessment Based on Eight Projects in Five New Jersey Cities," *Publius* 19 (Summer 1989): 107.

25. General Accounting Office, *Urban Development Action Grants—Effects of the 1987 Amendments on Project Selection* (Washington, D.C.: U.S. General Accounting Office, 1989), 2.

26. Department of Housing and Urban Development, Office of Community Planning and Development, *Report to Congress on Community Development Programs—1989* (Washington, D.C.: U.S. Department of Housing and Urban Development, 1989), 52.

27. Ibid., 54 and 58–59.

28. Department of Housing and Urban Development, *Analysis of the Income Cities Earn from UDAG Projects*, by David Rymph and Jack Underhill, (Washington, D.C.: U.S. Department of Housing and Urban Development, January 1990), 1.

29. International City Management Association, *Recycling CDBG and UDAG Funds* (Washington, D.C.: Management Information Publication–ICMA, January 1991), 1–2.

30. Rymph and Underhill, i.

31. John G. Heilman and Douglas J. Watson, "Publicization, Privatization, Synthesis, Tradition: Options for Public-Private Configurations," *International Journal of Public Administration* 16-1 (January 1993): 107–137.

32. Douglas A. Blackmon, "A Tale of Two Cities," *Atlanta Journal/Atlanta Constitution*, 22 November 1992, A1, A10, and A11.

33. Ibid., A10.

34. Clifford Krauss, "House Passes Aid Plan for Inner Cities," *New York Times*, 3 July 1992, A7.

35. Frank Shafroth, "Coalition Urges President Bush to Sign Aid Bill," *Nation's Cities Weekly*, 26 October 1992, 6.

36. Krauss, A7.

2

Targeting as Redistribution:
Does It Work?

A nationally developed policy of targeting intergovernmental aid assumes that the funds approved by a legislature for categories of places or people most in need, as determined by objective criteria, will actually get to the neediest places or people. The question of whether the funds in fact do so, or can be expected to do so, is thus a critical issue for redistributive policymaking.

The significance of this question is evident when one considers the enormous amounts of money transferred from federal to state and local governments and from state to local governments in the United States federal system. In 1950, federal grants to state and local governments were only $2.2 billion and represented one-tenth of federal domestic outlays. As late as 1964, annual federal grants totaled only $10 billion.

By 1980, sixteen years later, however, the federal budget contained $82.9 billion in grants to state and local governments. This amount comprised one-fifth of all federal domestic spending. By 1985, despite pressure from the Reagan administration to limit federal aid, the budget contained over $100 billion for states and localities.[1] By 1987, 24 percent of the revenue received by state governments and 38 percent of that received by local governments were raised by higher levels of government.[2] Despite a major change in the type of aid given, the element of targeting has been present in all these transfer programs. Richard P. Nathan points out that this growth in federal aid clearly outpaced inflation. In the process of growth, the "form of federal aid also changed."[3] In the 1970s, there was a movement away from categorical or project grants toward "larger, more flexible, and more automatic programs," such as block grants and revenue sharing.[4] The latter types of grants are also known as formula grants.

It might appear that this shift involved a movement away from targeting. Gary W. Copeland and Kenneth J. Meier explain a major difference between project and formula grants: "Formula grants provide no administrative discretion in the distribution of monies because agencies simply plug the relevant numbers into a congressionally determined formula and allocate funds accordingly."[5] Project grants, on the other hand, leave more discretion in the hands of administrative agencies to decide where the funds are to be spent.[6] While Congress specifies the targets it wishes to reach, the agencies have the responsibility to choose among the specific state or local government proposals that will receive the funds.

However, as Robert S. Montjoy and Laurence J. O'Toole point out, the question of targeting is very much a political one regardless of the type of grant utilized by Congress.[7] Under formula and project grants, Congress must decide the basic value choices of "whether targeting is important and, if so, which problems to target, which factors to include in the distribution decisions, and how much weight to give each factor."[8] Some have observed that agencies are not autonomous in the awarding of project grants but actually work to serve "the needs of the membership of Congress."[9] If that is true, then Congress has an equal ability "to put its mark on project grants" as it does on formula grants.[10] A project grant "defers and alters, but does not eliminate, the influence of narrow self-interest on the distributional process," Montjoy and O'Toole observe.[11]

TARGETING EFFECTIVENESS

In the past fifteen years, political scientists and economists have attempted to determine the success of intergovernmental grant programs in offsetting financial disparities among units of recipient governments. Thomas R. Dye states that a "principal rationale" for federal assistance has been "its assumed equalizing effect among jurisdictions."[12]

> Poorer state and local governments, serving larger proportions of needy persons—the aged, poor, and minorities—were assumed to benefit the most from redistributional effects of federal grants. By compensating for the lack of local resources and by directing federal aid to those jurisdictions confronting the most pressing demands, the federal grant-in-aid system was seen as a major equalizing mechanism and a guarantee of minimum nationwide levels of public service.[13]

Generally, allocation formulae include measures such as poverty level, average family income, unemployment rates, and other indicators of social need. The goal of targeting is to place the necessary resources in the hands of those who need assistance the most.

Targeting at the Federal Level

The research on targeting indicates that federal aid programs generally have not been successful in targeting resources to needy jurisdictions, although some researchers report moderate success in particular programs. Dye, who has been associated with much of the work in this research area, states strongly that federal aid targeting has been unsuccessful.[14] In one of the earliest (1978) works on targeting, Dye and Thomas L. Hurley find that variations in federal spending based on jurisdictional need are not statistically significant:

> No commonly accepted indicator of social need—size, growth rate, population density, black population percentage, aged population, female-headed households, room crowding, inadequate housing, age of city, death rate, crime rate, poverty, segregation, inequality, or even dependence on public assistance—accounts for more than 15 percent of total federal outlays.[15]

They conclude that state aid to cities is more effectively targeted than federal aid. That is, state aid is "more closely associated with size, growth rate, density, age of city, and segregation" than are federal grants.[16]

Peter D. Ward is critical of the methods used by Dye and Hurley in reaching their conclusion that federal aid is not effectively targeted.[17] He believes that Dye and Hurley's use of per capita measurements distorts the concept of responsiveness that Dye and Hurley attempt to gauge.[18] Ward's analysis indicates that "aid allocations are driven exclusively by population size."[19] This finding is sufficient, in his view, to establish that targeting is indeed successful.

In a critical response to Ward, Dye writes that "cities with more people do indeed receive more dollars in aid. Now if this fact satisfies our concept of 'targeting' to social needs, then we need not proceed further in our analysis. But most social scientists will view such information as trivial."[20]

The debate over the use of per capita data has extended beyond the work of Dye and Hurley. Robert M. Stein and Keith E. Hamm, in commenting on Ward's criticism of Dye and Hurley, question "whether there was ever a problem in need of correction."[21] In defending their own use of per capita data, Stein and Hamm state, "By using a per capita aid measure, we are controlling for population size when studying targeting effects."[22]

Targeting at the State Level

Other researchers who have compared federal and state aid and generally have agreed with Dye and Hurley that state aid is more effective in targeting than is federal aid. A 1979 National Governors Association (NGA) study concludes, clearly from a self-serving viewpoint, that the states are closer to the problems of cities and can be more effective in targeting funds to them. Of course, the authors of the NGA study want federal funds to continue to flow, but to the states rather than directly to the cities.[23]

While finding that state targeting is more effective than federal, Stein reports that state assistance is related to needs criteria only in a handful of states. The finding that only nine states consistently channeled funding to the neediest communities illustrates the wide variation in targeting among states. Furthermore, Stein criticizes Dye and Hurley for using aggregate-level analysis that assumes there are no differences among the states in the manner in which they distribute funds to subunits.[24] The majority of states exhibit no tendency toward targeting. Stein finds that this failure by Dye and Hurley to recognize the differences among state aid systems and to use pooled analysis of all states' aid led them to erroneous generalizations.[25]

John P. Pelissero, after examining state aid to the nation's forty-seven largest cities, believes that states have been "very responsive to some common indicators of city need."[26] Pelissero agrees with Ward's criticism of per capita measurements that total aid and population will necessarily be highly correlated. He finds that population explains 81 percent of the state aid received by cities in 1962 and 77 percent of that received in 1976. Pelissero concentrates on the residual aid, that is, "the 19–23 percent of state aid that is determined by factors other than population."[27]

Pelissero employs regression analysis to determine bivariate correlations between state aid to cities and three separate dimensions of city need—social need, economic need, and fiscal need. Social needs are represented by such indicators as crime, unemployment, and percentage of elderly population. Economic needs are judged on the bases of population density and homeownership. The fiscal need dimension is represented by budget deficit, debt burden, fiscal effort, and functional inclusiveness (city responsibility for education and/or welfare services).[28] Pelissero finds that a combination of fiscal need and social need measures explains 80 percent of residual state aid in 1962 while social, fiscal, and economic measures explain 90 percent of state aid in 1976.[29]

Using the same methods to analyze data for cities over 300,000, Pelissero reports in a second journal article that states were responsive to city needs in two functional areas—welfare and education—in 1962 and again in 1976. Pelissero states that the findings in these functional areas "provide some support for the aggregate studies of state aid responsiveness to city needs."[30] He finds that targeting by states for education aid based on need improved from 1962 to 1976 but, in the case of welfare aid, "the pattern often seemed to be toward higher allocations to less needy cities."[31]

Pelissero's work is limited to sixteen cities in his analysis of education targeting and eighteen cities in welfare targeting. Stein and Hamm point out that limiting the analysis of targeting to very large cities may bias the results since the proportion of people in need and city fiscal plight are positively related to city size.[32] Also, Pelissero's work may be questioned for using very small sample sizes, which is a persistent criticism of targeting research in general.

Others do not agree that states have been effective in targeting aid to needy communities. Paul D. Moore studied general-purpose aid in New York State that was supposed to be "needs-based." He reports that funds were distributed to "every community, not just a targeted few."[33] Moore predicts that state lawmakers will eliminate a remaining needs-based program, which Moore claims is a forerunner to General Revenue Sharing, in favor of "categorical programs for which they can take some credit."[34]

Susan B. Hansen contrasts targeting of economic development aid by economic sector and by geographic area. She finds that New York State has been successful in sectoral targeting because it has emphasized the fostering of technological change rather than the saving of failing industries. However, Hansen reports:

> By contrast, aid to declining regions, central cities, the poor, or the long-term unemployed is usually allocated by legislatures, where partisan and territorial interests are very much involved. While representation of such interests fulfills important political functions, efficiency is not among them. State aid is either diluted too much to have an impact, or wealthier areas commanding superior political resources received a disproportionate share.[35]

Frank J. Mauro and Glenn Yago also find that targeting of economic development aid in New York State has not been effective. They see much of the reason for failure "related to the fact that there is not popular, professional, or political consensus as to the objectives that state economic development programs should pursue or the programmatic approaches likely to secure particular objectives."[36] Specifically, Mauro and Yago conclude that support for targeting for manufacturing industries remained strong despite further decline of this sector. Very interestingly, however, state efforts to target distressed areas did not persist, for they were expanded to statewide, nontargeted programs as a result of political pressure. One program remained targeted to distressed areas for only five years and the other for nine years. Commenting on the expansion of one of those programs, the Job Incentive Program, Mauro and Yago observe that "the program fulfilled neither its original targeted objectives during its early years nor its comprehensive objectives in its subsequent expanded form."[37]

Proposed Explanations for the Failure of Targeting at the Federal Level

While the evidence on the ability of states to target funds based on need is mixed, there appears to be consensus in the literature that federal programs have not been successful in targeting. Stein and Hamm state that "federal aid allocations exhibit no evidence of targeting" after examining aid data on 35,000 municipal governments in 1977 and in 1982.[38] Dye declares their results "the most authoritative in the field."[39]

Two general reasons are often given for the inability of the federal government to target aid effectively: one emphasizes evenness of outcome, on population or geographical bases; the other emphasizes politics. Discussions in the literature may emphasize one explanation more than the other. For instance, Copeland and Meier determine that federal grants are allocated to local governments almost wholly on the basis of population.

> In no case can per capita income, percent of families in poverty, tax effort, unemployment rates, urbanization, or age of the housing stock explain as much variation as population. In fact, none of these variables adds more than 6% of explained variance to the population figure.[40]

As previously mentioned, Pelissero finds that population explains approximately four-fifths of the state aid received by cities in 1962 and 1976.[41]

Others who have tried to explain the lack of targeting have tended to focus on overt political reasons. Stein and Hamm believe that because federal lawmakers are free of requirements for balanced budgets, they tend to "universalize" the distribution of federal grants because it is advantageous to incumbents.[42] Similarly, Kenneth A. Shepsle and Barry R. Weingast argue that legislator uncertainty leads to universalism as the norm in Congress so that members can demonstrate to constituents what they "have done for them lately."[43] Michael J. Rich cites works that "argue that legislators prefer programs that allocate benefits broadly, including something for (almost) everyone as opposed to programs that concentrate benefits in a few select districts."[44]

The literature just reviewed thus develops two categories of explanations for the failure of federal aid targeting: (1) federal funds are distributed primarily on the basis of population, and (2) Congress' desire to universalize federal grants for political purposes negates the effectiveness of targeting.

These two explanations are related in practice. The simplest method for Congress to universalize federal grants is to distribute them on the basis of population. Targeting certainly cannot be successful if there is constant political pressure to distribute grant funds based on population. These literature-based explanations suggest that the failure of targeting can be explained by a theory of politics and political processes. The next section explores this possibility by relating the empirical research on targeting to the existing theoretical literature on policy types.

THEORY OF POLICY TYPES

A thorough review of the literature on targeting of intergovernmental fiscal aid illustrates clearly the lack of a theoretical basis for the work published. With some exceptions, notably the work of Rich,[45] the research is heavily empirical with little effort to relate the important concept of targeting to a broader theoretical literature. Researchers cited in the prior section have used various techniques to correlate different need measurements of cities to the amounts of aid received. If the correlation was significant, then researchers concluded that targeting was effective. More often than not, no positive correlation was found.

Lowi's Theory of Policy Types

An important body of literature is available to explain, in the context of a political theory, the results found in the targeting literature. This literature focuses on the issue or concept of policy types, and has grown from the seminal 1964 work of Theodore Lowi.[46] Lowi developed a typology of public policies with three major categories: distribution, regulation, and redistribution. Distributive policies involve those in which government benefits are distributed without regard for limited resources, for they are "disbursed almost on a basis of come one, come all."[47] Lowi states that "patronage" can be taken as a synonym for "distributive."[48] Robert R. Lineberry identifies distributive policies as "pork barrel" projects for all constituencies.[49] According to Lowi, distributive policies are "virtually not policies at all but are highly individualized decisions that only by accumulation can be called a policy. They are policies in which the indulged and the deprived, the loser and the recipient, need never come into direct confrontation."[50]

Regulatory policies are, stated in general terms, applicable to a designated sector of the economy. Individuals are "affected by the law in roughly the same way."[51] Unlike distributive policies, regulatory policies cannot be disaggregated to the individual level because of the general application of broader law. Regulatory policies are "usually disaggregable only down to the sector level."[52]

Policies that are redistributive take resources from one person or group and give them to another. Lineberry observes that the commodity most often redistributed is money, but it can also be status or political power.[53] The categories of those impacted by redistributive policies are generally very broad, approaching social classes, according to Lowi. He elaborates: "They are, crudely speaking, haves and have nots, bigness and smallness, bourgeoisie and proletariat. The aim involved is not use of property but property itself, not equal treatment but equal possession, not behavior but being."[54] Lowi later concludes that redistribution issues "cut closer than any others along class lines and activate interests in what are roughly class terms."[55]

The choice among these policy types is not politically neutral. Congress prefers distributive policies because "[w]hen a billion-dollar issue can be disaggregated into many millions of nickel-dime items and each item can be dealt with without regard to the others, multiplication of interests and of access is inevitable, and so is reduction of conflict."[56]

The coalition necessary to pass legislation involving a distributive policy is based on what E. E. Schattschneider called "mutual non-interference."[57] By that, Schattschneider meant that it is acceptable for each player to seek benefits for himself but to neither support nor oppose benefits for others. In Schattschneider's classic discussion of rivers and harbors, the terms "logrolling" and "pork barrel" are presented. Lowi argues that these terms have not been given enough serious study. They provide insight into the development of distributive policies: "A logrolling coalition is not one forged of conflict, compromise, and tangential interest but, on the contrary, one composed of members who have absolutely nothing in common; and this is possible because the 'pork barrel' is a container for unrelated items."[58] If policies can be disaggregated, patronage can be spread and conflict can be avoided.[59]

Redistributive policy issues contrast with distributive issues in other critical ways. In redistributive issues there are only two sides, "and the sides are clear, stable, and consistent."[60] The sides are understood by Wallace Sayre's designations of "money-providing" and "service-demanding" groups.[61] The conflict around redistributive issues becomes institutionalized to the point that national party leaders, administrations, and even segments of the bureaucracy identify with one side or the other. Lowi contends that Congress cannot effectively balance redistributive issues because they "require complex balancing on a very large scale" and Lowi claims that Congress is not capable of doing that.[62] Decision making is done within the bureaucracy and by other upper-class leaders who are "holders of the 'command posts.'"[63] In other words, the congressional politics of redistributive policies are highly unstable, and the politics of distributive policies are relatively stable.

Lowi believes that redistributive programs result in two sides forming—one around those that provide the funds and one around those that receive the funds. Furthermore, and very important, Lowi predicts that the resolution of this conflict is either to make a redistributive program more distributive or to abolish it, for Congress is not capable of the "complex balancing" required to maintain a redistributive program.[64]

Building on Lowi's Theory

Since Lowi's seminal work in 1964 and his later revisions, there have been a number of efforts to criticize, refine, or alter it. Some of these efforts are directly relevant to the research issue at hand. For example, Randall B. Ripley and Grace A. Franklin concur that there are only two sides on redistributive issues, a "pro" (liberal) position and a "con" (conservative) position. They argue the usefulness of this terminology:

> "Liberal" and "conservative" may not be highly pleasing labels to potential theorists, but to participants in the political process dealing with redistributive issues, they have meaning in the sense that the same two coalitions usually emerge for any measure in dispute, whether it be medicare or aid to the disadvantaged in a variety of forms or civil rights or even procedural issues that have important implications for the handling and resolution of redistributive issues in the future.[65]

Policies that tend to aid the disadvantaged in this country are generally considered redistributive while policies aiding groups that are already advantaged are perceived as distributive, according to Ripley and Franklin.[66] This difference in perception means that policies proposed to aid disadvantaged individuals or groups "always set off major political rows."[67] Usually there are ideological and/or partisan issues involved that render reaching agreement on redistributive policy proposals very difficult.

Ripley and Franklin use examples of how Congress reached agreement on four major redistributive issues only after redefining them to emphasize their distributive characteristics. In an important insight for the present purpose, Ripley and Franklin note:

> The attainment of redistributive policy is achieved at a cost of diluting its impact by adding or emphasizing distributive elements. Programs that are purely redistributive are virtually impossible to enact. Programs that have distributive elements broaden the base of support and both camouflage and reduce the redistributive elements. The pressures to redefine controversial redistributive proposals as distributive continue after original passage is secured. Both implementation and subsequent reauthorizations are often the occasions for attempts to broaden the number or type of beneficiaries beyond the most disadvantaged.[68]

Michael T. Hayes refines Lowi's typology by distinguishing "between consensual and conflictual demand patterns, thus stressing the importance of political opposition."[69] The key for a group or a coalition of groups seeking allocative benefits from Congress is to "keep the relationship among active participants non-zero sum and cooperative by drawing the spoils from unorganized groups not active on the issue."[70] In this way, there are no losers because potentially conflicting interests can be satisfied through logrolling.[71]

Conversely, in the redistributive arena, Hayes notes that "Congress actually makes an explicit choice among contending groups."[72] Redistributive policy choices result in winners and losers so both sides "are attentive and aware of the stakes, thus making the legislative conflict inherently zero-sum in form."[73] The important variable for Hayes is the demand pattern that gives rise to either a distributive or redistributive decision.

The theory of policy types based on Lowi's seminal work is still developing. The hundreds of references to Lowi's 1964 article suggest the usefulness of his typology to public policy theorists. It can also be useful to those researchers concerned with the question of targeting of intergovernmental grants. Lowi and those who built on his work offer theoretical arguments that can be used to explain the findings of the empirical research done on targeting. A major theme in the targeting literature is that for various reasons Congress desires to universalize the distribution of federal grants. Redistributive programs that target disadvantaged groups tend to be very divisive, as Ripley and Franklin point out. Lowi and others have argued that Congress is not capable of maintaining support for redistributive programs once they become divisive.

Targeted programs are redistributive and, as the evidence in the literature illustrates, are subject to the problems Lowi and others have described for redistributive policies. As stated earlier, the research on targeting has been primarily empirical in nature. However, greater understanding of the success or failure of targeted, redistributive programs can be gained when they are placed in the context of the literature on the theory of policy types. Targeted programs will fail in that either the political support needed to maintain them will force them to become less targeted (redistributive) or they will lose support and die. This general expectation is tested here with respect to the Urban Development Action Grant (UDAG) program.

UDAG TARGETING

The Urban Development Action Grant program was specifically intended to target the nation's most distressed and most impacted cities through selective investment in private sector projects that would create new jobs and taxes. Section 119(a) of the enabling legislation makes it clear that UDAGs were targeted "to severely distressed cities and urban counties to help alleviate physical and economic deterioration through reclamation of neighborhoods having excessive housing abandonment or deterioration, and through community revitalization in areas with population outmigration or a stagnating or declining tax base."[74] An important question, then, about UDAG for public managers and policy makers, as well as for academicians, was whether the Department of Housing and Urban Development (HUD) was successful in reaching truly distressed communities according to its definition of the criteria for distress and impaction and through its selection formula.

The question of targeting is especially appropriate in the case of the Urban Development Action Grant program because UDAG was intended to be a highly targeted effort.

Objects of Targeting

UDAGs were projected to target resources in three different ways:

1. *Needy Places*—A review of early discussions in Congress and presentations by the Carter administration make it clear that UDAG was intended to assist "severely distressed" urban areas. Very important for present purposes, the original concept was for UDAGs to be used to help the larger, older rustbelt cities that were not competitive economically with the suburbs or newer sunbelt cities.[75] As older factories closed down, jobs left the cities and myriad problems—white flight, crime, drugs, poor education, housing—remained.

2. *Needy People*—Numerous references in the legislation and in congressional hearings were made to the need for UDAG to assist

low- and moderate-income residents of distressed urban areas.[76] The fact that UDAG was enacted as an amendment to the Community Development Block Grant (CDBG) program emphasizes the intent of Congress to assist low- and moderate-income residents.

3. *Projects*—The initial legislation mandated that HUD spend its UDAG appropriations equally on three types of projects—industrial, commercial, or housing (neighborhood).[77] The requirement to target equally by type of project was removed by Congress in 1981 at the request of the Reagan administration. Later attempts by the administration to remove housing as an eligible project type were defeated in Congress by advocates who remembered that one of UDAG's primary missions was to rehabilitate failing neighborhoods. However, by the end of the program the Reagan administration had successfully changed the focus of UDAG to economic development, primarily commercial development in the large cities.[78]

While all these forms of targeting are important, the emphasis of this study is on the UDAG program's effectiveness in targeting the distressed urban places in the United States. While the literature in general has shown that the federal government is not effective in targeting aid to local governments, the research on the effectiveness of the UDAG program is mixed on the targeting question. As the following review shows, of the seven studies found in the academic literature on UDAG targeting, three conclude that the UDAG program was effective in reaching the most distressed and impacted cities and urban counties, one is critical of UDAG's level of success, and three others reach mixed conclusions.

Research Literature on UDAG Targeting

In analyzing data supplied by the Department of Housing and Urban Development (HUD), John R. Gist finds that "the selection process has worked relatively well in targeting severely distressed cities."[79] Gist arrives at this conclusion by accepting HUD's data showing that two-thirds of the grants to large cities went to the 40 percent categorized as most distressed. He suggests that the addition of the "pockets of poverty" category to the UDAG program was a "dilution of the targeting emphasis of the program and a concession to opponents in Congress to gain passage of UDAG in the FY 80 budget."[80]

Gist and R. Carter Hill reach an opposite conclusion. They developed a model replicating the decision process used by HUD in approving UDAG applications, and using the same criteria HUD used in defining the levels of distress and impaction of eligible cities.[81] Gist and Hill's database consists of the 114 large city applications evaluated by HUD in the first funding cycle in 1978. They conclude that no "distress measures specified in regulations dealing with the program were statistically significant in explaining the awarding of grants."[82] Their model suggests that the more highly distressed cities actually have a lower chance of receiving funds.[83] The only variables linked to funding in the Gist and Hill model are the level of private commitment and the ratio of private funds to the entire project amount.

Two other studies produced positive results on the question of UDAG's targeting effectiveness. One of these studies was performed by Jerry A. Webman, and the other was completed by Ingrid W. Reed. Webman concludes that "the most distressed cities did receive a disproportionate share of grants," based on his review of HUD-provided data on 520 grants awarded between April 1978 and January 1980. In Webman's analysis, the most distressed quartile of cities received almost four times as many grants as the least distressed quartile.[84] In dollar terms, he estimates that for the "typical" city of 500,000, the monetary difference in UDAG receipts for the most distressed city compared with the least distressed city is $2.9 million over the two program years he examines.[85] Using regression analysis, Webman concludes that "total UDAG funds are strongly related to the impaction index when population is held constant."[86] He also utilizes eight case studies of UDAG projects in five New Jersey cities in reaching his conclusions.[87]

Ingrid Reed's study strongly suggests that UDAG was effective in helping the most distressed cities compete with their wealthier neighbors. She evaluates eight UDAG projects in New Jersey and, on that limited basis, concludes that "private investment was attracted to depressed urban areas."[88] She credits UDAG with allowing these eight distressed communities to compete with the wealthier suburban communities to which development was quickly moving. Reed quotes one New Jersey developer:

> Most development going on is not in the cities. It's in the suburbs. Land is cheaper, highways are better, and that's where the tenants seem to want to be. Like any industry, the real estate industry is basically going to do what its market tells it to do.[89]

Reed sees UDAG as one tool the distressed cities were able to use to counter the broader economic and social trends described earlier.

Rich draws mixed conclusions from his study of the distributional impacts of the UDAG program using multiple regression analysis. Rich regressed separately the number of action grants, total action grant dollars, and action grant dollars per capita on population size, region, level of prior HUD experience, need, and private investment.[90] Although he finds that nearly two-thirds of the large city projects were awarded to cities in the most distressed quartile, he concludes that the level of private funds committed and population size were better predictors of UDAG selection success than was the degree of distress. However, "need remains a significant predictor of action grant outcomes when population, region, prior experience, and private investment are controlled for."[91]

Interestingly, he suggests that "the relative influence of politics in the action grant sweepstakes warrants further investigations."[92] Rich recommends: "Of particular interest may be the relative influence of congressmen (for example, key committee members). It may be that HUD officials seek to build and maintain support for their program by funding a number of small projects in as many districts as possible."[93] Rich offers no empirical evidence of political interference in the UDAG selection process, however.

In a later study of urban aid, including UDAG, Rich reaches a number of interesting conclusions using cross-sectional regression analysis. First, he finds that the numerous measures of community need utilized by scholars and government agencies generally produce the same list of the neediest cities.[94]

Second, and most important for the present discussion, most federal urban aid is distributed to the cities most in need although "allocations among cities within the most distressed group were not very responsive to the level of city need."[95] This mixed finding in targeting is of special interest because it introduces the notion of examining targeting within the neediest portion of eligible cities, and reflects the importance of reaching the truly neediest cities.

Third, Rich finds that the federal government's ability to target cities most in need increased over time from the 1950s to the 1980s.[96] Fourth, local demand for UDAG program funds was positively correlated with the distribution of federal aid. The more times a given city filed applications for funding, the more funds it was likely to receive.[97] Finally, in response to the question he posed in his earlier study, Rich concludes that "political influence . . . accounted for little in the distribution of program funds."[98]

Yong Hyo Cho and David Puryear analyze the targeting effectiveness of several urban aid programs, including UDAG, by employing four different distress measures, two of which are the "Urban Development Action Grant Distress Ranking" and the "Urban Development Action Grant Impaction Ranking." Cho and Puryear find that UDAG fails to target its resources on cities with the most need based on any of the distress measures. They do point out that because only a limited number of cities are even eligible to participate in the UDAG program, UDAG is "highly targeted on distressed cities in the absolute."[99] However, among eligible cities, the distress measures have little correlation with funding patterns.

This discussion raises a theme that will be revisited in the analysis: different standards can be introduced for assessing targeting effectiveness. These range from the straightforward problem of whether eligibility criteria were applied, to the more complex issue of the extent to which the neediest among the eligible cities received more support than did the cities that were less needy, but still eligible.

SUMMARY AND CONCLUSION

Redistributive policies generate conflict because they transfer something of value from one group or location to another. These policies revolve around class differences and the ensuing conflict almost always involves taking from the haves and giving to the have-nots. Because of the conflict inherent in redistributive programs, smooth implementation is very difficult to achieve.[100] Distributive policies are less likely to cause conflict because there is something in them for every constituency. Lowi uses the terms "logrolling," "patronage," and "pork barrel" to describe distributive policies.

Congress is not comfortable with redistributive programs because each elected representative has to demonstrate to his or her constituency that he or she can "bring home the bacon." The tendency is for redistributive programs with strong ideological bases to become more distributive, if they survive at all. Mauro and Yago, in their study of targeting in New York State, report that state programs targeted to distressed areas were expanded to statewide nontargeted programs because of political pressure.[101] Ripley and Franklin state that the conflict over redistributive policies puts pressure on politicians and bureaucrats

> to shift the program away from strict redistribution to the less well-off and to make it a program that serves a broader clientele or one that, in effect, becomes distributive and offers advantages for many groups, including those who are politically more influential and for whom, therefore, help is less controversial.[102]

Ripley and Franklin offer convincing arguments on the conversion of several major programs from redistributive to distributive. The War on Poverty, the Economic Development Administration, and the Comprehensive Employment and Training Act (CETA) are three of the examples used.[103] A fourth program is the Community Development Block Grant (CDBG), which has become primarily a distributive program.[104] CDBG's funding formula is biased in favor of the suburban communities and not the distressed cities. A "relatively small proportion of the program's funds go to the poorest geographical areas."[105] This resulted from the fact that CDBG is a formula grant with use of the funds defined only in terms of permissible activities.[106]

In the 1970s and 1980s, conservative administrations advocated distributive programs, such as General Revenue Sharing and the various block grant programs. Redistributive project grants of the 1960s, such as urban renewal, neighborhood development, Model Cities, water and sewer facilities, and the numerous War on Poverty programs, were eliminated in favor of the distributive programs of the 1970s and 1980s.

Because the Urban Development Action Grant program was a major exception in the 1970s to the trend toward formula grants, the issue of its success in targeting is interesting in both theory and practice. UDAG was a project grant program targeted originally for the large, distressed urban areas of the country. It was enacted partly in response to the loss of funding these cities experienced when the categorical/project grants of the 1960s were replaced by the CDBG program.

According to the theory developed in this chapter, UDAG should have faced numerous efforts to make it more distributive so that its funds could be spread across many congressional districts regardless of need. If this happened, UDAG would survive, even if in a different form, because of the broad political support it would generate based on its assistance to more than just the neediest of urban jurisdictions. Conversely, if it failed to become more distributive, it would perish because too many federal and local officials would have seen no benefit to their constituents in supporting UDAG.

In either case, regardless of whether UDAG succeeds, targeting fails. In the first instance, the population-based explanation of targeting failure applies because the program becomes so diluted it loses effectiveness as a targeted program. In the second scenario, the policy-based explanation applies because support for continuing the program is closely tied to the direct benefits received from it. If the policy of allowing only the neediest jurisdictions to apply for funds were to be maintained, political opposition would lead to its demise.

Within this theoretical framework, the situation of program administrators is fraught with tension, especially if they are committed to the redistributive outcomes their programs are designed to accomplish. The UDAG case is particularly interesting in this regard. As a project grant program, UDAG was the exception to the trend in the 1970s and 1980s toward formula grants as the vehicle for federal aid to local governments. Formula grants do not have to be distributive, as opposed to redistributive, but they usually are. The reason may be that the political pressures for universalization are more immediate with formula grants. The consequences are obvious to all and there will not be another chance short of an amendment.

Project grants, by contrast, defer decisions to agencies and change the forum in which individual representatives seek benefits for their constituencies. For a while, all may hope to win, or at least to get their fair share under this new game. But over time, if the program is truly targeted—in response to a mandate from Congress acting as a whole—the allocation decisions will necessarily displease a large number of individual members in their capacities as district representatives. If the impetus that stimulated the original passage wanes, as it frequently does, then the program may be left without support in future budgetary battles. The direction of political pressure can change without any change in the statute.

Agency officials are surely aware of this problem, and so they are placed in a dilemma. They can remain true to their mandate and risk losing support. Alternately, they can try to maintain support by distributing benefits more widely, thereby undermining the targeting intent of the original mandate.

A mixed strategy is also possible among complex and ever-changing power relationships. It has long been noted that organizations often pay attention to inconsistent goals by addressing them sequentially. An agency faced with the targeting/logrolling issue may attempt to serve both goals. That is, it can devise ways to satisfy some distributional demands while maintaining as much targeting as possible under the circumstances.

In this case the agency would have the added burden of justifying its actions to, or hiding them from, the original beneficiaries. The ability to use smokescreens may be enhanced by extremely complex decision rules.

If these processes are truly at work in our political system, then we would expect to find evidence of them in the UDAG program because the benefits of the program were both highly visible and geographically specific, thereby creating pressure for representatives to play the role of district advocates.

We know, of course, that the program eventually was terminated. The continued decline of American cities rules out mission accomplishment as a rationale for its retirement. We believe that a review of the history of UDAG will reveal evidence of the political processes outlined above.

NOTES

1. Michael J. Rich, "Distributive Politics and the Allocation of Federal Grants," *American Political Science Review* 83–1 (March 1989): 193.

2. Robert S. Montjoy and Laurence J. O'Toole, "Policy Instruments and Politics: Multiple Regression and Intergovernmental Aid," *State and Local Government Review* 23-2 (Spring 1991): 51.

3. Richard P. Nathan, "The Politics of Printouts," in *The Politics of Numbers*, eds. William Alonso and Paul Starr (New York: Russell Sage, 1987), 331.

4. Ibid.

5. Gary W. Copeland and Kenneth J. Meier, "Pass the Biscuits, Pappy: Congressional Decision Making and Federal Grants," *American Politics Quarterly* 12 (January 1984): 8.

6. Ibid.

7. Montjoy and O'Toole, 51.

8. Ibid.

9. Copeland and Meier, 9.

10. Ibid.

11. Montjoy and O'Toole, 53.

12. Thomas R. Dye, *American Federalism: Competition Among Governments* (Lexington, Mass.: Lexington Books, 1990), 112.

13. Ibid.

14. Ibid.

15. Thomas R. Dye and Thomas L. Hurley, "The Responsiveness of Federal and State Grants to Urban Problems," *Journal of Politics* 40 (February 1978): 206.

16. Ibid., 204.

17. Peter D. Ward, "The Measurement of Federal and State Responsiveness to Urban Problems," *Journal of Politics* 43 (February 1981): 83.

18. Robert M. Stein and Keith E. Hamm, "A Comparative Analysis of Targeting Capacity of State and Federal Intergovernmental Aid Allocations: 1977, 1982," *Social Science Quarterly* 68 (September 1987): 451.

19. Ibid.

20. Thomas R. Dye, "Targeting Intergovernmental Aid," *Social Science Quarterly* 68 (September 1987): 445.

21. Stein and Hamm, 451.

22. Ibid.

23. John P. Pelissero, "State Aid and City Needs: An Examination of Residual State Aid to Large Cities," *Journal of Politics* 46 (August 1984): 918.

24. Robert M. Stein, "The Allocation of State Aid to Local Governments: An Examination of Interstate Variations," in *State and Local Roles in the Federal System*, Advisory Commission on Intergovernmental Relations (Washington, D.C.: U.S. Government Printing Office, 1982), 203.

25. Ibid.

26. Pelissero, 931.

27. Ibid., 925.

28. Ibid., 926.

29. Ibid., 931.

30. John P. Pelissero, "Welfare and Education Aid to Cities," *Social Science Quarterly* 66 (June 1985): 451.

31. Ibid.

32. Stein and Hamm, 451.

33. Paul D. Moore, "General Purpose Aid in New York State: Targeting Issues and Measures," *Publius* 19 (Spring 1989): 30.

34. Ibid., 31.

35. Susan B. Hansen, "Targeting in Economic Development: Comparative State Perspectives," *Publius* 19 (Spring 1989): 60–61.

36. Frank J. Mauro and Glenn Yago, "State Government Targeting in Economic Development: The New York Experience," *Publius* 19 (Spring 1989): 82.

37. Ibid., 80.

38. Stein and Hamm, 461.

39. Dye, 444.

40. Copeland and Meier, 7–8.

41. John P. Pelissero, "State Aid and City Needs," 925.

42. Stein and Hamm, 462.

43. Kenneth A. Shepsle and Barry R. Weingast, "Political Preferences for the Pork Barrel: A Generalization," *American Journal of Political Science* 25 (February 1981), 110.

44. Rich, 195. See also Mauro and Yago, 82.

45. Ibid., 193–213.

46. Theodore J. Lowi, "American Business, Public Policy, Case-Studies, and Political Theory," *World Politics* XVI-4 (July 1964): 677–715.

47. Robert R. Lineberry, *American Public Policy: What Government Does and What Difference It Makes* (New York: Harper & Row, 1978), 97.

48. Lowi, 690.

49. Lineberry, 97.

50. Lowi, 690.

51. Ibid., 691.

52. Ibid.

53. Lineberry, 97.

54. Lowi, 691.

55. Ibid., 707.

56. Ibid., 692.

57. Ibid., 693.

58. Ibid.

59. Ibid., 693.

60. Ibid., 711.

61. Ibid.

62. Ibid., 715.

63. Ibid.

64. Ibid., 715.

65. Randall B. Ripley and Grace A. Franklin, *Congress, the Bureaucracy, and Public Policy,* 4th ed. (Chicago: Dorsey Press, 1987), 145.

66. Ibid., 146.

67. Ibid.

68. Ibid., 175.

69. Michael T. Hayes, *Lobbyists and Legislators* (New Brunswick, N.J.: Rutgers University Press, 1981), 27.

70. Ibid., 30.

71. Ibid., 29.

72. Ibid., 33.

73. Ibid.

74. *Housing and Community Development Act of 1977, Statutes at Large*, 91, sec. 119(a) (1977).

75. Congress, House, Committee on Banking, Finance, and Urban Affairs, *Housing and Community Development Act of 1977*, 95th Cong., 1st Sess., 24 February 1977, 17–49.

76. Ibid., 34.

77. *Housing and Community Development Act of 1977, Statutes at Large*, 91, sec. 119(j) (1977).

78. The focus of UDAG was shifted during the Reagan years to commercial projects. The bulk of the commercial UDAGs (88 percent) went to the construction of hotels, motels, inns, malls and shopping centers, office buildings, recreation facilities and sales centers, and restaurants. Director of the Office of Management and Budget David Stockman told Congress:

> From an economic viewpoint, these are all necessary and worthy kinds of investments, responsive to marketplace demands, but there is no conceivable national interest justification for their continued inclusion in a Federal budget.

Stockman's point was that UDAG should have been targeted to foster technological change or to help American industries to be more competitive internationally. (See Congress, Senate, Committee on Banking, Housing, and Urban Affairs, *Housing, Community Development, Mass Transportation Authorizations—1986: Hearing before the Subcommittee on Housing and Urban Affairs*, 99th Cong., 1st Sess., 15 April 1985, 783.)

79. John R. Gist, "Urban Development Action Grants: Design and Implementation," in *Urban Revitalization*, ed. Donald B. Rosenthal (Beverly Hills: Sage Publications, 1980), 250. See also Michael J. Rich, "Hitting the Target: The Distributional Impacts of the Urban Development Action Grant Program," *Urban Affairs Quarterly* 17-3 (March 1982): 295.

80. Ibid., 251.

81. John R. Gist and R. Carter Hill, "The Economics of Choice in the Allocation of Federal Grants: An Empirical Test," *Public Choice* 36-1 (1981): 68.

82. Ibid., 72.

83. Ibid., 72.

84. Jerry A. Webman, "UDAG: Targeting Urban Economic Development," *Political Science Quarterly* 96-2 (Summer 1981): 202.

85. Ibid., 204–205.

86. Ibid., 202–203.

87. Ibid., 199–200.

88. Ingrid W. Reed, "Life and Death of UDAG: An Assessment Based on Eight Projects in Five New Jersey Cities," *Publius* 19 (Summer 1989): 104.

89. Ibid., 95.

90. Rich, "Hitting the Target: The Distributional Impacts of the Urban Development Action Grant Program," 295–298.

91. Ibid., 298.

92. Ibid., 299.

93. Ibid.

94. Rich, "Distributive Politics and the Allocation of Federal Grants," 204.

95. Ibid., 205.

96. Ibid.

97. Ibid., 206.

98. Ibid., 207.

99. Yong Hyo Cho and David Puryear, "Distressed Cities: Targeting HUD Programs," in *Urban Revitalization*, ed. Donald B. Rosenthal (Beverly Hills: Sage Publications, 1980), 209.

100. Randall B. Ripley and Grace A. Franklin, *Bureaucracy and Policy Implementation* (Homewood, Ill.: Dorsey Press, 1982), 158.

101. Mauro and Yago, 82.

102. Ripley and Franklin, 174.

103. Ibid., 163–172.

104. Ibid., 165–167.

105. Ibid., 167.

106. Ibid., 166.

3

Political History of the UDAG Program:
The Role of Targeting

This chapter reviews the origins, development, and demise of the Urban Development Action Grant (UDAG) program. Consistent with the discussion at the end of Chapter 2, emphasis is placed on those actions that sought to broaden UDAG in order to maintain majority support in Congress and blunt UDAG's effectiveness as a targeted program. The political history of UDAG is especially important for the lessons it holds for other targeted federal programs. It provides a partial test of whether a program initially targeted to limited geographic areas can maintain a national constituency large enough to survive.

During its eleven-year life, the Urban Development Action Grant program was the subject of considerable political controversy. Some opposition to UDAG was based on its mandated purpose to target only severely distressed urban areas. HUD's definition of what qualified as a distressed community tended to favor the older cities of the Northeast, Mid-Atlantic, and North Central regions of the country. Representatives in Congress from the West and South felt UDAG was not benefiting their regions and wanted the program's scope broadened or the program eliminated. Substantial evidence will be presented in this chapter and Chapter 4 that supports this assertion.

Others opposed UDAG on ideological grounds. New structural and financial arrangements between the private and public sectors resulted from the UDAG program, including a proactive economic development function in local government. UDAG emphasized public investment in activities that are generally considered to be in the domain of the private sector, and therefore was considered an unwelcome intruder in the private marketplace. Certain critics argued that UDAG was not large enough to make a real difference in the creation of new investment and, thus, was a waste of money. Further, some critics considered UDAG an unnecessary subsidy to developers who would have built their projects even if they had not received UDAG assistance.

On the other hand, proponents argued that UDAG was an unqualified success. Officials of numerous cities believed UDAG was the catalyst that gave them an advantage in attracting major development projects to their cities. Businesspeople generally supported UDAG as a tool that enabled them to invest in projects they claimed they would not otherwise undertake. Testimonials to UDAG's role in revitalizing some of America's oldest central cities were common in the popular literature of the 1980s. Some observers argued that the urban crisis could be solved only through a new public-private partnership modeled on the UDAG program.

The pressure on UDAG advocates seeking to maintain at least majority support in Congress was great. At each reauthorization, and in later Reagan administration budgets, UDAG opponents called for its termination. As a result, UDAG's scope was broadened in different ways to make it appealing to a larger constituency. Based on the targeting literature, one might expect that these broadening measures would lessen UDAG's effectiveness as a targeted program for large, "severely distressed" cities.

EARLIER FEDERAL REDEVELOPMENT PROGRAMS

By the 1960s, America's larger cities were clearly in trouble. Racial strife, white flight, crime, failing public education, and crumbling public and private infrastructure were topics of great concern.[1] The federal government invested billions of dollars through numerous different programs to combat urban ills. One of the early attempts at redevelopment was Urban Renewal, which was similar to UDAG in several respects. Another precursor to UDAG was the Economic Development Administration's (EDA) Title IX program.

The Housing Act of 1949 authorized grants to local governments to acquire and remove blighted areas for reuse through sale to private developers or for the construction of public housing.[2] Later congressional enactments of Urban Renewal emphasized the purchase and clearing of blighted areas for redevelopment by the private sector. The worst slums were often found near downtown areas so the property on which the buildings were located had potentially high economic value. John C. Bollens and Henry J. Schmandt observe:

> By demolishing the slums, space would be made available for industrial and commercial expansion and, more importantly, for middle-

and high-income housing that might lure back some of the city's former residents, the consumers and taxpayers of substance who had fled to the greener pastures of suburbia.[3]

For commercial projects, cities were required to file applications with the Renewal Assistance Administration outlining their plans to redevelop designated blighted areas. The federal government paid for two-thirds of the cost of purchasing the property, assembling smaller parcels into larger tracts, relocating inhabitants, clearing the existing structures, and building new infrastructure necessary for redevelopment by the private sector.[4] The major difference between Urban Renewal and UDAG was found in the timing and certainty of the private investment. Under Urban Renewal, the land was placed in a developable state, following the steps mentioned above, before a private commitment to redevelop it was made. UDAG, however, required a firm financial commitment in advance through contractually binding agreements. Other differences included UDAG's more overt intention to create jobs and increase local tax revenue.[5]

EDA's Title IX program and UDAG were similar in that both targeted economically distressed communities.[6] However, EDA's emphasis was on assisting cities with short-term high unemployment whereas UDAG's distress and impaction criteria sought to identify cities faced with long-term deterioration, as well as immediate economic problems. Gist notes also that EDA's program did not seek to leverage[7] private funds but rather other public funds.[8]

By the 1970s, there was such a large amount of federal funds going to cities that some observers feared cities had become dependent on federal funds.[9] The buildup of federal funds resulted from President Nixon's New Federalism initiatives to create block grants from the numerous Great Society categorical programs and from President Carter's 1977 "economic stimulus package, which substantially expanded funding for public service jobs, local public works, and countercyclical revenue sharing."[10] James W. Fossett notes that federal aid to cities increased by nearly 700 percent during the 1970s.[11]

By the mid-1970s the nation was suffering from "stagflation"—both high unemployment and high inflation rates. Cities were especially hard hit because it was clear that the white flight to suburbia Bollens and Schmandt described was not limited to housing. Reed notes that jobs and retail activity were also drawn away from the cities, "leaving them with declining populations and financial resources."[12]

As part of the urban strategy of the federal government in the 1970s, economic revitalization was seen as essential to the long-term health of the nation's cities. The other tactics of funding public service jobs and public works projects were viewed as short-term solutions to immediate economic crises. The Carter administration envisioned the Urban Development Action Grant program as "a form of government intervention to deal with perceived market imperfections in economically disadvantaged cities."[13] The "market imperfections" Carter recognized revolved around the failure of the private sector to invest in decaying inner cities because of the perceived high financial risk as well as the high cost of real estate. President Carter saw private investment induced by federal funds through UDAG as a major hope for revitalizing distressed cities.

EARLY LEGISLATIVE HISTORY

The first mention of the UDAG program before Congress was contained in the presentation by Secretary of Housing and Urban Development Patricia Roberts Harris before the Subcommittee on Housing and Community Development of the House Committee on Banking, Finance, and Urban Affairs on February 24, 1977. Harris, presenting the month-old Carter administration's program for Fiscal Year (FY) 1978 for the Department of Housing and Urban Development, stated that in the summer of 1976 President Carter had promised the United States Conference of Mayors an urban policy responsive to the needs of America's cities— "their needs for coordinated economic development, their needs for housing and the services to sustain the people who would inhabit that housing."[14] The primary initiative to implement Carter's urban economic development policy was UDAG. Harris testified that HUD

> currently lacks the capacity to respond adequately to cities faced with the greatest physical decline and economic deterioration. . . .
> Current block grant funding levels provide hardest-hit cities only enough resources to carry out maintenance-level activities or to complete existing projects. Few cities can launch major new initiatives under the program as it is currently structured. Furthermore, the Department has no flexible funding system to respond to special development opportunities as they arise. When the right combination of circumstances arises, local government, like a business, must be able to move quickly to take advantage of investment opportunities and market conditions.[15]

Harris envisioned that the proposed action grants would assist "severely distressed cities" to eliminate the deterioration they faced in two ways: (1) specific economic development targeted to sections of cities that were losing population and tax base; and (2) "reclamation projects" in residential sections that suffered from severe problems of abandoned and dilapidated housing.[16] Harris told the Committee members that

UDAG would be special or unique because it would "stimulate new and increased private investment while establishing private sector confidence that will protect current investment."[17]

The Carter administration, then, projected UDAG as an opportunity to target funds to severely distressed cities and, more particularly, to the neighborhoods hardest hit. In her testimony Harris cited three examples of projects UDAG could be used to fund, and all three involved attracting private investment into dying downtowns or decaying residential neighborhoods.[18]

Harris also pointed out that cities that did not have a good record in providing housing for low- and moderate-income families and employment opportunities for minorities would not be eligible for UDAG through an application process that would, among other things, require them to show their track records in equal opportunity efforts in housing and employment.[19] Apparently none of the larger urban areas, which were otherwise eligible, failed to meet these requirements.

The response from interest groups and from members of Congress was generally favorable to the proposed UDAG program. The National League of Cities (NLC) applauded Secretary Harris for proposing a program that would "aid severely distressed communities who are experiencing economic hardship."[20] The level of annual funding recommended ($400 million) for the first three years was thought inadequate by NLC but it supported "the general thrust of the program" and hoped more funding would be appropriated in the future.[21]

James Williams, testifying for the National Association of Regional Councils, supported Harris's emphasis on the inclusion of economic development as a major component of the Carter administration's HUD strategy.[22] He saw UDAG as an opportunity to revive dying central cities with funds to combat the "cheaper land and less stringent requirements of the suburbs."[23] Williams concluded: "Government and private development must work together, and it may be the kind of innovation which HUD would like to see will show disbelievers that such a partnership can work for both the public and private interest."[24]

William L. Slayton, executive vice president of the American Institute of Architects, endorsed UDAG as "the $400 million initiative to aid particularly distressed cities."[25] Slayton, the Urban Renewal Commissioner in the Kennedy and Johnson administrations, urged the panel not to allocate UDAG by entitlement, but by judgment of HUD officials based on which cities could best use the funds.[26]

The American Federation of Labor & Congress of Industrial Organizations (AFL-CIO) told Committee members that housing construction and rehabilitation were not enough to restore the economic vitality of the older American cities.[27] It supported the administration's proposal but urged that UDAG be used only where "specific arrangements for retention or expansion of jobs are involved."[28] Now that government had built an extensive infrastructure in the nation's cities, it was important to attract businesses to use that infrastructure. UDAG could be the vehicle to create jobs in distressed cities, the AFL-CIO believed.

During the congressional hearings and debates, voices were also raised in opposition to the concept of UDAG. Some of the issues that would lead to UDAG's later political troubles were discussed. Not everyone agreed with the administration's proposal to aid large distressed cities, especially targeting the inner cities rather than the suburbs. Furthermore, many of the most distressed areas were located in the Northeast and Midwest. Political support for UDAG as proposed was not broad enough to ensure passage because UDAG appeared to target large rustbelt inner cities. Representatives from Southern and Western states and those with suburban and small city constituencies saw little in the program to justify their support.[29] In the later years of the UDAG program, this perceived bias toward large Northeastern and Midwestern cities led to major changes in the program in an effort to maintain support from Southern and Western members of Congress.

During the congressional debates on UDAG, a concern was expressed that UDAG was simply a return to the pre-CDBG (Community Development Block Grant) categorical grants, particularly Urban Renewal. A minority amendment offered to, and rejected by, the full House Committee on Banking, Finance, and Urban Affairs stipulated that the first $3.5 billion appropriated would go to full funding of CDBG, the next $100 million to close out all ongoing Urban Renewal projects, and finally, if funds were available beyond $3.6 billion, up to $400 million to UDAG.[30] In its report, the minority believed UDAG costs would escalate uncontrollably like many Urban Renewal projects, which averaged close to $14 million each.[31]

The minority members concluded:

The UDAG proposal and the proposed tighter review of the regular CDBG program, which is to be administratively proposed, are disconcerting to us since individually and collectively, they suggest a trend by the administration to return to the categorical, "Washington has to approve, Washington knows best," syndrome—the very thing the 1974 act was intended to prevent.[32]

Senator John Tower (R-TX) argued against UDAG as a "modified Urban Renewal Program" and as duplicative of the CDBG program.[33] Furthermore, Tower believed the growing metropolises of the sunbelt, such as Atlanta, Miami, and Houston, would never receive UDAG funds because of the bias toward the older Northern cities.[34] Even though he was wrong (most of the large sunbelt cities benefited to some degree from UDAG), Tower hit a sensitive nerve that plagued UDAG throughout its existence.

Two substantial changes were made to the UDAG proposal that broadened its base of support prior to its adoption. First, urban counties over 200,000 population were added to the list of potentially eligible local governments by the Senate, even though many urban counties contained the suburban communities that early proponents complained were harmful to the older central cities.[35] The Senate Committee on Banking, Housing, and Urban Affairs found "some urban counties may possess the same kinds of distress factors found in metropolitan cities" and deserved to compete for the funding.[36]

Second, smaller cities were included in the UDAG legislation under Section 119(k): "Not less than 25 percentum of the funds made available for grants under this section shall be used for cities under fifty thousand population which are not central cities of a standard metropolitan statistical area." By the end of the program, over 10,000 small cities were eligible for UDAG. Over 8,000 of the eligible small cities had populations less than 2,500 and half of those had under 500 citizens.[37]

Smaller cities presented a challenge to the HUD staff in the early years because of the lack of local staff capability and awareness. HUD developed an extensive effort through workshops and written communications to advise small city officials about UDAG.[38] In the first years of the program, HUD held two funding rounds each quarter of the fiscal year for applications to be submitted with four of the eight rounds dedicated exclusively to the receipt and consideration of small city applications. HUD's attention to small cities allowed it to reach its 25 percent set-aside by the end of the program.

LOCAL GOVERNMENT MODELS FOR UDAG

As with many innovations in federal and state programs, the model for UDAG can be found in successful local programs, such as the Philadelphia Industrial Development Corporation (PIDC). The PIDC was founded in 1958 as a joint venture of the City of Philadelphia and the Greater Philadelphia Chamber of Commerce and as a quasi-public non-profit development corporation with board members from both the city and the business community.[39] The Philadelphia program emphasized industrial, commercial, and neighborhood development through the leveraging of private investment by the use of relatively small amounts of public money, some of which came from Community Development Block Grant funds and some from city coffers.[40]

Walter D'Alessio, executive vice president of PIDC, explained the theory on which PIDC had been operating for nearly twenty years before UDAG was introduced:

> Economic development efforts are centered around providing capital in the form of loans and equity investment in local business and manufacturing enterprises in order to support job creation and pump needed capital into the area's business sector. Local businesses which lease space in the new commercial center are supported by loans from the corporation. . . .[41]
>
> Realistically, there will never be sufficient public funds to alone reverse the trends of deterioration found in most major urban centers. Leveraging of private investment to accomplish this objective is absolutely essential, and the best way to achieve that is through the federal support of local development institutions capable of the coordinated use of resources in the framework of investment rather than expenditure.[42]

The Philadelphia program was only one of several brought to the attention of federal officials through a study prepared by the National Council for Urban Economic Development (NCUED) under contract with HUD. The contract for the study was signed two years before UDAG was introduced by Secretary Harris. Specifically, NCUED was charged with exploring the linkages among federally funded development programs, such as EDA, CDBG, and CETA, in cities. And, more important, HUD wanted to know how public-private partnerships could be developed to leverage private investment in economically depressed cities.[43]

The results of these studies of successful local public-private efforts of urban revitalization led to the creation of a coordinated development demonstration program for ten large cities. HUD, EDA, and Labor provided each city with up to $500,000 for two years to develop coordination linkages among public and private sources to achieve targeted development through leveraging of public funds.[44] The reports of these leading local programs, such as the one in Philadelphia, confirmed to HUD the legitimacy of the role of federal funds in creating economic development opportunities in distressed cities.

UDAG AS AN INDEPENDENT PROGRAM

UDAG was envisioned by its early advocates as a supplement to the Community Development Block Grant program passed in 1974. It was intended specifically to support economic development. While economic development by cities was an allowed activity under the Housing and Community Development Act of 1974, there were several barriers to its use. NCUED found that economic development was not encouraged in the CDBG regulations and administrative guidelines.[45] The orientation of CDBG was largely toward "public expenditures" to address housing and infrastructure needs in neighborhoods. By contrast, economic development requires "public investment" to leverage private sector capital in the creation of new jobs.[46] CDBG's objectives, then, were not consistent with those of local economic development programs, such as Philadelphia's.

A major impediment to the use of CDBG funds for economic development was in the local political control of the money, according to NCUED.[47] Researchers found that elected officials were inclined to "spread the funds fairly thinly among the many constituencies and neighborhoods vying for assistance."[48] Economic development projects requiring large investments of public funds fared poorly in the competition with well-organized neighborhood groups demanding infrastructure improvements.

In addition, CDBG funds are distributed on a "draw down" basis, which means that funds for local governments are released by HUD as expenditures are made. As a consequence, cities had difficulty using the CDBG funds as leverage with local bankers to secure more favorable terms for low-income loans because the funds could not be acquired before actual expenditures were made, NCUED found.[49]

A third problem was that the CDBG management staff at HUD did not consider revitalization of the urban economic base to be its mission.[50] NCUED cited the administrative decision not to allow the capitalization of local development corporations with CDBG funds as an example of an anti-economic development attitude by CDBG staff members.

The Carter administration concluded that a new program with clearly stated economic development goals was needed to overcome the political and bureaucratic barriers found in CDBG at the time. The concept of UDAG had been explored by HUD through its contract with NCUED and the ten model programs it had established two years prior to the Carter administration. HUD found ready acceptance of the UDAG proposal from President Carter and Secretary Harris. Changes made later in the CDBG legislation and regulations encouraged large cities and states, on behalf of small cities, to use CDBG funds more extensively for economic development purposes.

IMPLEMENTATION DURING THE CARTER YEARS

One top UDAG staff member labeled the first three years during the Carter administration as the "honeymoon" period because of the strong support for the program from the administration.[51] President Carter was proud enough of the one major initiative in urban policy credited to his administration to the point he invited all UDAG staff members in 1979 to meet with him in the Rose Garden.[52] Furthermore, the program received overall strong congressional support as evidenced by an amendment in December 1979 to increase its appropriation for FY 1980 and FY 1981 to $675 million per year.

HUD moved quickly after passage to implement the UDAG program with the first project grant awards announced in June 1978. In FY 1978, 236 applications were approved with the number increasing to 285 in FY 1979 and to 416 in FY 1980.[53] Fifty-five percent of the applications received in the first three years eventually were funded.[54] Approximately one-third of the projects went to each of the eligible categories—commercial, industrial, and neighborhood—although nearly twice as much money was granted for commercial projects as for either industrial or neighborhood projects.[55]

By the end of the Carter administration, considerable enthusiasm for UDAG existed within HUD, as evidenced by the Department's reports of accomplishments in developing public-private partnerships to create economic development. For example, HUD told Congress that many UDAGs were focusing on the conversion of old industrial plants to new uses:

> A former Ford automobile assembly plant in Somerville, Massachusetts will become Assembly Mall, a large commercial complex. Waterloo, Iowa has rehabilitated an abandoned freight depot into a restaurant and retail shop, while Hammond, Indiana will be able to install necessary improvements to transform the abandoned Erie Railroad switching yards into a residential development. An abandoned factory in Hartford, Connecticut will be converted into residential units and commercial spaces, as will the historic Woolen Mill in Winooski, Vermont.[56]

In addition, numerous other examples of using UDAGs to keep industries from leaving large urban areas were cited. HUD attempted to illustrate how UDAGs were being used effectively in the early years to intervene in the private market to affect locational and investment decisions. Presumably without UDAG assistance, normal market decision making would have resulted in new factories or retail malls locating in suburbia or elsewhere in the country.

The early direction given the UDAG program by the Carter administration was not substantially altered in later years. The emphasis on public investment in the private market had a basically positive reaction from those who had seen the failure of urban programs of the prior twenty years. The Reagan administration attempted to expand other initiatives to develop public-private partnerships that began with UDAG.[57]

ADDITION OF POCKETS OF POVERTY

An obvious attempt to broaden UDAG's political appeal was the addition of the "pockets of poverty" category in the Housing and Community Development Amendments of 1979. Metropolitan communities and small cities that did not meet the distress and impaction criteria for eligibility were able to apply if they had areas within their communities meeting certain distress thresholds.[58] Congress stipulated that up to 20 percent of all UDAG funds could go to pockets of poverty applicants.

For a metropolitan community to have an eligible pocket of poverty, it had to have a contiguous area containing at least 10,000 persons (2,500 persons for small cities) or 10 percent of its population; at least 70 percent of the residents of the pocket of poverty must have had incomes below 80 percent of the local median income; and at least 30 percent must have had incomes below the national poverty level, as determined by the Office of Management and Budget (OMB).[59]

In addition, pockets of poverty applicants had to prove that they had provided housing for low- and moderate-income citizens as well as equal opportunity in employment and housing for low- and moderate-income persons and minority groups.[60] The community seeking a pockets of poverty Action Grant also had to meet the following requirements:

- It was to provide 20 percent match to the grant funds.
- No less than 75 percent of the new jobs from the project had to go to low- and moderate-income persons.
- At least 51 percent of the jobs had to be provided to residents of the pocket of poverty.
- Twenty percent of the jobs were to go to persons eligible for the Comprehensive Employment and Training Act (CETA) program, who were long-term unemployed, underemployed, or from low- and moderate-income families.
- It had to prove that the benefits of the UDAG were related to the needs of the low- and moderate-income residents of the pockets.[61]

The pockets of poverty amendment did not result in a large amount of money going to the otherwise noneligible cities. Only fifty-nine pockets of poverty grants were awarded through FY 1988 out of the nearly 3,000 total approved projects by HUD. The fifty-nine projects represented $116 million, or less than 3 percent, of the $4.6 billion approved in UDAG funds.[62]

SUPPORT AND OPPOSITION TO UDAG WITHIN THE REAGAN ADMINISTRATION

The first major HUD analysis of the UDAG program was commissioned by HUD Secretary Samuel Pierce upon taking office in 1981. He explained in the Foreword to the study issued in January 1982:

> Soon after becoming Secretary of HUD, I directed Steve Savas, my Assistant Secretary for Policy Development and Research, to conduct a major evaluation of the Urban Development Action Grant (UDAG) program. A study was necessary because there was no systematic information on how well this program was doing its job, which would enable me to reach an informed decision whether the program was worth keeping.[63]

The Savas study, which recommended the continuation of UDAG, turned out to be a major factor in extending the life of UDAG, for Secretary Pierce became a strong advocate for the program as a result. Pertinent details of the Savas study recommendation will be presented in the next chapter. The primary opposition in the new administration to UDAG was formidable: it appeared in the person of David Stockman, the director of the Office of Management and Budget.

Stockman, in his *Triumph of Politics*, wrote about his strong dislike for UDAG:

> If there was a single program in the 1981 budget we inherited that was both a statist abomination and something a Republican Administration had a chance to kill outright, it was the Urban Development Action Grant Program. It was called UDAG—a sincere-sounding acronym that covered a multitude of sins. PORK would have been more accurate.
>
> It had been started in 1978 by the Carter Administration, and had quickly ballooned to a cost of $650 million a year. During the '80 campaign, the Carter people had used it for blatantly political purposes.
>
> UDAG was a classic example of the single-entry bookkeeping fallacy. The spenders said that by subsidizing downtown hotels and ski resorts, the federal government would "create" jobs and "redevelop" lagging local economies. What they didn't say was you would also raise taxes, waste savings, and destroy jobs paying for it. On any conservative hit list, this would be right at the top.
>
> Or so I thought. But Secretary of Housing and Urban Development Sam Pierce launched a noisy campaign to spare this turkey, and soon

the White House switchboard was flooded with HUD-orchestrated "distress calls" from local Republican mayors and "businessmen" who happened to be in the redevelopment and construction business.

With unsettling rapidity, they convinced Ed Meese that UDAG was really a "Republican program"—never mind that it had been started during the Carter Administration—because the grants had to be leveraged with private capital. I told both Meese and Pierce that this kind of "leveraging" was an old trick in the federal spending game. Other federal grants could be used to "leverage" UDAG deals. It was a good case, in fact, of the double fleece.

To no avail. Meese ordered me to restore the program and told me in no uncertain terms that taking it to the President would be of no use. It took some time for it to sink in that the Counselor of the supposedly most ideologically conservative President of the twentieth century had decided not to touch perhaps the most ideologically offensive and wasteful bit of federal spending on the block.[64]

Secretary Pierce acknowledged the importance of the Savas study in achieving the support of the new administration's appointed officials in HUD and for its role in convincing President Reagan to maintain UDAG.[65] An official HUD document summarizing the achievements of HUD under Pierce described a critical event after the Savas study:

The next step was to present the case, as HUD saw it, in favor of keeping the program. At a meeting with the President, the Secretary of HUD and the Director of OMB presented their cases for and against, respectively, retaining UDAG. The President decided to retain it. The UDAG program was subsequently authorized at the lower figure of $435 million [sic] and included in the Omnibus Budget Reconciliation Act of 1981.[66]

Key UDAG staff members did not understand Stockman's persistent strong opposition to the program. First, as a congressman from Michigan, Stockman pressured HUD to fund UDAG applications in his district. Second, staff members realized the idea for UDAG was actually conceived in the Republican Ford administration and not the Democratic Carter administration. Third, the UDAG program was small when viewed in relation to the total federal budget or even as a percentage of the $14.9 billion HUD budget. And last, ideologically, UDAG was close to the new administration's theory of trickle-down economics in which investment by the wealthy was encouraged while the benefits of new jobs and taxes would "trickle down" to the masses.[67]

In 1985 testimony before the Senate Subcommittee on Housing and Urban Affairs of the Committee on Banking, Housing, and Urban Affairs, Stockman urged the panel to terminate UDAG for several reasons. He argued: (1) UDAG served no clear national purpose because most of the funds were being used for local commercial development; (2) UDAG is not targeted effectively to low- and moderate-income citizens; (3) UDAG's claims of leveraging large sums of private capital are "misleading and largely incorrect"; and (4) the national economy is improving so rapidly that UDAG is not needed to generate new jobs. UDAG produced less than 1 percent of the new jobs created in the economic expansion of the early 1980s, Stockman claimed.[68]

In an earlier publication, further insight is found into the reasons for Stockman's strong dislike for UDAG. He said, "When you have powerful underlying demographic and economic forces at work, federal intervention efforts to reverse the tide turn out to have rather anemic effects."[69] His opposition to UDAG apparently was based on the belief that government's attempts to influence market decisions through direct investments were bound to have little substantial effect.

CHANGES IN UDAG DURING THE REAGAN ADMINISTRATION

Several important changes were made in the UDAG program in the years of the Reagan administration to make UDAG more distributive and less targeted to the large cities of the rustbelt. These broadening measures were both legislative and administrative ones. Members of Congress whose districts were not benefiting directly from UDAG viewed UDAG as an expendable program unless it could be made less redistributive.[70] UDAG advocates within HUD knew that the program would survive only if it benefited cities throughout the country and not just in the rustbelt.[71] The focus of UDAG was also changed from targeting aid to specific distressed urban areas to helping the nation recover from the recession of the early 1980s. The result was less emphasis on targeting the social ills of the large cities through the creation of new housing and other neighborhood projects and more on the creation of investment and jobs in communities suffering from the recession.

Reasonable Balance Rule

In the Housing and Community Development Amendments of 1981, Congress reduced the appropriation for UDAG for FY 1982 and FY 1983 from $675 million to $440 million. More important, it revised the requirement that there must be a "reasonable balance" among industrial, commercial, and neighborhood types of projects. In conjunction with this change, the purpose of the program was focused to "concentrate on stimulating economic development activity to aid in economic recovery."[72]

When the 1977 Act was passed, the reasonable balance requirement was seen as a vehicle to encourage neighborhood groups with relatively small projects to participate in UDAG.[73] Paul K. Gatons and Michael Brintnall report that small cities preferred to submit industrial project applications and large cities preferred large-scale commercial projects.[74] As a result, HUD announced that it would consider neighborhood projects separately and not in competition with industrial and commercial projects in order to generate neighborhood projects. Furthermore, the classification for neighborhood projects was intentionally broadened: "if they were predominantly housing (wherever located), commercial outside the central business district, sponsored by a neighborhood-based organization (whatever the activity or location), or if they somehow benefited residents of a specific 'neighborhood.'"[75] By the beginning of the Reagan administration, HUD had achieved the "reasonable balance" by awarding sufficient numbers of UDAGs to neighborhood projects.

The 1981 amendments led to a gradual decline in the funding of neighborhood projects. In FY 1981, one-third of the projects were classified as neighborhood; in FY 1982, one-fourth; and in FY 1983, one-fifth.[76] Specifically, Reagan's HUD wanted to discourage housing projects that did not create permanent jobs. The 1981 amendments had shifted the intent of the program strongly to economic development; housing projects were not considered consistent with this new objective.[77] Presumably, cities with commercial and industrial growth would benefit more than cities without growth since a higher percentage of the UDAG appropriation could now be used for commercial and industrial projects.

With the change in the reasonable balance requirement in 1981, UDAG funding went proportionately in greater amounts to large city commercial projects and small city industrial projects.[78] By the end of the program, housing projects had received only 11 percent of the funds and 15 percent of all project awards.[79]

1982 Program Changes

Revised UDAG Regulations were published in the *Federal Register* effective March 31, 1982, to reflect the 1981 amendments.[80] The major changes were as follows:

1. The major purpose of UDAG was altered so as "to stimulate recovery in severely distressed communities."[81] Specifically, the new Regulations read: "(a) The purpose of urban development action grants is to assist cities and urban counties which are experiencing severe economic distress to help stimulate economic development activity needed to aid in economic recovery."[82]

This statement of purpose is interesting for two reasons: (a) UDAG's role in economic development was stressed. It was seen as an antirecessionary tool to create jobs. No mention was made of social targeting, such as aiding low- and moderate-income people or providing adequate housing; (b) the emphasis was placed on cities experiencing "severe economic distress" in contrast to cities suffering from "physical distress." The 1977 authorizing legislation and the HUD formulae for eligibility and project selection gave heavy weight to the factors of physical distress, which are discussed in detail in the next chapter. The 1982 statement of purpose was an apparent effort to change the direction of UDAG to an economic stimulus program for all cities suffering from the recession of the 1980s regardless of physical problems, as represented by the impaction criteria.

2. Requirements for a written citizen participation plan, a community development plan, and a Housing Assistance Plan were eliminated, even though public hearings were still required. UDAG was also exempted from the A-95 procedure which required all grant applications to be reviewed and commented on by local and state agencies or "clearinghouses."[83]

3. Guam, the Virgin Islands, and Indian Tribes were added to the list of jurisdictions eligible to apply for UDAG funding.[84]

1983 Program Changes

In 1983, HUD attempted to eliminate all purely housing projects from the UDAG program. Housing, under the draft regulations, would be allowed only in mixed-use projects and if it could be proven to create permanent jobs.[85] The reaction in Congress to the draft regulations was extremely negative; the result was quick withdrawal by HUD. The House of Representatives even went so far as to restore the "reasonable balance" rule. However, the final 1983 amendments stated only that HUD "may not discriminate among programs on the basis of the particular type of activity involved, whether such activity is primarily a neighborhood, industrial, or commercial activity."[86]

1984 Program Changes

During FY 1984, HUD revised the UDAG Regulations to lessen the number of funding rounds per year from eight to six. Rather than a quarterly funding cycle, HUD scheduled a large city/urban county round and a small city round every four months. While this change lengthened the time it took a city to receive approval on a proposed project, HUD justified its action:

> The revised funding cycle provides applicants and private parties participating in the projects more time to complete and refine their applications. The revision also gives more time between each funding round for HUD to prepare contracts and amendments to grant agreements and to work with applicants to improve the quality of grant applications.[87]

Another important change in 1984 was the addition of a seventh criterion for UDAG eligibility—the Labor Surplus Area (LSA). The classification of LSA was given by the Department of Labor to high-unemployment centers for the purpose of targeting federal procurements. An area became an LSA automatically if it exceeded 120 percent of the national average unemployment rate over the prior two years. HUD stated in the *Federal Register* that it added LSA as a seventh criterion out of the concern expressed by members of Congress over "the severe unemployment rates being experienced in particular areas."[88] It quoted extensively from the congressional debate on the "explicit congressional interest in linking the UDAG program more directly to problems of unemployment."[89] HUD exempted this new rule from all notice and public comment requirements in order to implement it immediately.

Adding the LSA criterion resulted in a major broadening of eligibility for UDAG. HUD estimated that 14 large cities and 1,800 small cities would become eligible.[90] The impact of having a seventh criterion was probably even greater than HUD expected. Prior to the rule change, HUD listed 365 eligible large cities. The next list following the rule change showed 412 eligible large cities.

One other action was taken that received little notice anywhere. In 1984, at the height of the criticism over the use of the pre-1940 housing criterion, HUD reduced the threshold requirement for pre-1940 housing from 33.98 percent to 21 percent. In other words, to gain a point for pre-1940 housing toward eligibility, a city or urban county had to have only 21 percent of its housing built prior to 1940. No explanation accompanied the change in this requirement nor was it noted by HUD or the General Accounting Office (GAO) in their various reports to Congress. When combined with the addition of the Labor Surplus Area as a seventh criterion, the lowering of the pre-1940 housing percentage was an important change in the formula. It is probably not coincidental that the number of eligible cities increased from 365 in 1982 to 412 in 1984. Table 3-1 was developed from the minimum standards of physical and economic distress requirements for UDAG published periodically in the *Federal Register* and illustrates this major change, as well as other less important ones.

TABLE 3-1

Minimum Standards of Physical and Economic Distress for UDAG Eligibility

	1978	1980	1981	1982	1984	1986	1987
Age of Housing	35.15% or more	33.77% or more	33.88% or more	33.98% or more	21.0% or more	20.8% or more	20.2% or more
Per Capita Income	$1424 or less '69-'74	$1762 or less '69-'75	$2694 or less '69-'77	$2683 or less '69-'77	$4036 or less '69-'77	$5467 or less '69-'81	$6203 or less '69-'73
Population Lag/Decline	15.52% or less '60-'75	16.68% or less '60-'77	17.78% or less '60-'79	19.82% or less '60-'80	20.7% or less '60-'80	23.9% or less '60-'82	25.3% or less '60-'84
Unemployment	6.98% or more 1977	5.95% or more 1978	5.64% or more 1979	7.24% or more 1981	9.4% or more 1982	7.0% or more 1984	6.5% or more 1986
Job Lag/Decline	7.08% or less '62-'72	7.08% or less '67-'72	6.74% or less '72-'77	6.75% or less '72-'77	6.9% or less '72-'77	3.4% or less '77-'82	3.3% or less '77-'82
Poverty	11.24% or more 1970 Census	11.07% or more 1970 Census	10.92% or more 1970 Census	10.87% or more 1970 Census	12.4% or more 1980 Census	12.3% or more 1980 Census	12.3% or more 1980 Census
Labor Surplus Area					10% or more Unempl. '81-'82	10% or more Unempl. '82-'83	10% or more Unempl. '84-'85

1985 Program Changes

In January 1985, the Secretary of HUD issued in the *Federal Register* a clarification to the statutory provision that UDAGs could not be used to assist industrial or commercial businesses moving from one distressed city to another. The policy statement made it clear that projects would not be funded if they had the effect of relocating jobs and if that relocation had "an adverse [effect] on the unemployment or economic base of another distressed area . . . from which the jobs might be relocated."[91]

The impetus for renewed emphasis on the requirement against using UDAG to relocate industries came from rustbelt congressmen who believed UDAG was being used to lure industries from their districts to the South. Specifically, the House Committee on Banking, Finance, and Urban Affairs directed the General Accounting Office to investigate a December 1984 UDAG to Wilmington, North Carolina, to relocate the American Hoist and Derrick Company from St. Paul, Minnesota. GAO concluded that the manufacturing plant was a relocation and that HUD was negligent in not enforcing the "antipirating" provision of the 1977 UDAG law.[92]

1986–1988 Program Changes

Despite President Reagan's early support for UDAG and for Secretary Pierce in his confrontation with OMB Director Stockman, the Reagan administration proposed the elimination of the UDAG program for FY 1986. Disregarding the administration's recommendation, Congress, through the 1986 Appropriations Act, authorized $330 million for UDAG. The Housing and Urban-Rural Recovery Act of 1983 had earlier authorized $440 million for FY 1986. However, after Gramm-Rudman-Hollings Act cuts were made, UDAG ended up with an appropriation of $315.8 million.[93] A top UDAG staff member believed the importance of this reduction was that it led to undermining of support for UDAG in the cities and in Congress.[94] City officials no longer believed UDAG had the necessary resources to be of significant assistance.

The last attempt to garner support for UDAG from the South and West was found in the 1987 amendments. Based on complaints that these regions were not getting their fair share of UDAG, Congress divided the available funds, establishing a "two-pot" system in which all projects competed for 65 percent of the funds in the first pot based on the existing formula. From the second pot, consisting of the other 35 percent of the funds, projects were selected on the basis of project merits only (see Table 3-2). The purpose of this change was to achieve a wider geographic distribution of the funds and, concomitantly, broader political support for the program.[95]

TABLE 3-2

**Elements Comprising Project Merit Points
for UDAG Applications***

Elements	Points
Leveraging Ratio	10
UDAG Dollar per Job	6
Total New Permanent Jobs	2
Percent Hour/Moderate Income Jobs	1
Percent Minority Jobs	1
Percent CETA Jobs	1
Tax Benefits per UDAG Funds	1
Retained Jobs	1/2
Construction Jobs	1/2
Impact on Physical Development	1/2
Impact on Economic Development	1/2
Timeliness	1
Demonstrated Performance	1
Relocation	1
Minority Business Participation	1
Energy	1
State and Local Funds	1
Total	30

*Source is internal HUD document, undated.

The appropriation for UDAG was reduced in 1987 to $225 million.[96] Funds were again reduced in FY 1988 to $216 million and no new funds were appropriated by Congress for FY 1989. Unfortunately, UDAG had been weakened by the constant battering from the administration and the shrinking appropriations from Congress to the point that the 1987 changes were too little too late. UDAG was eliminated despite the numerous efforts to broaden its political appeal.[97]

THE DEATH OF UDAG

In 1987, President Reagan attacked UDAG in a major speech and demonstrated publicly that he, like Stockman, did not believe that UDAG was serving a worthwhile role in economic development. Reed quotes Reagan's comments to the 1987 annual meeting of the National Association of Counties: "The UDAG program, he complained, has provided 'millions to build luxury hotels, restaurants, and fancy condominiums.' On the latter, he quipped, 'I barely had time to discover what yuppies were, until Congress began to subsidize them.'"[98] Reagan also criticized UDAG in his 1989 budget message and specifically cited a UDAG for a $13.6 million hotel project in St. Petersburg, Florida, as unnecessary.[99]

The *New York Times* announced the death of UDAG on June 30, 1988, by reporting that Congress had taken the "oh-so-rare step of killing a costly federal program that has provided great political advantage to many members of Congress."[100] In the context of the gradual decline in funding for UDAG from its high-water mark of $675 million in 1980, it is not surprising that funding for the program finally dwindled to zero. Reed observes, "the fact that the program survived 8 years of attacks by the Reagan administration meant that the fatal blow at the hands of Congress could be seen as a *coup de grace* rather than a *coup d'etat.*"[101]

Newspaper accounts of the budget deliberations in June 1988 agree that UDAG was "traded off" for continuation of the NASA space station program.[102] The HUD budget was included in a package with NASA and fifteen other agencies.[103] The decision in Congress apparently came down to funding one program or the other and, as the *Nation's Cities Weekly* headline read, "Congress kills UDAG for space dreams."[104] The *Congressional Quarterly* reported that some congressmen were disappointed that the 1987 amendments were not working to redistribute UDAG funds.

Citing *Congressional Quarterly* sources, Reed observes

that Neal Smith (D-IA), a sub-committee member "who had supported the (formula) change because it was designed to help states like his, said that it wasn't having its desired effect, anyway, so he supported the cut." Rep. Edward P. Boland (D-MA), chairman of the appropriations subcommittee and a defender of UDAG for years, called UDAG the "lowest priority." In addition, Rep. Bill Green (R-NY) a long-time supporter of UDAG, obviously saw the end in sight and said, "Frankly, I think it's time to call it quits."[105]

Despite a few attempts by members of the HUD-Independent Agencies Subcommittee to save UDAG, the full subcommittee voted down each effort to delete funds from the NASA budget for UDAG. When the Conference Committee on the budget met on August 2, 1988, no one in Congress attempted to revive UDAG.[106]

UDAG finally succumbed for a number of reasons, almost all of them political in nature. First, the Reagan administration, except for HUD Secretary Pierce, White House Counsel Ed Meese in Reagan's first term, and early support from the president, opposed the concept of UDAG and attempted to eliminate or downsize it continuously. Second, the effort through the 1987 amendments to broaden its political appeal, contrary in part to its original purpose, did not have the desired effect. Third, the dwindling appropriations and the lengthened review time both made UDAG less appealing to developers and cities. Apparently, UDAG supporters were simply worn down, as Representative Green's statement indicates, and they realized UDAG was not worth fighting for any longer.

RAMIFICATIONS

The history of the UDAG program suggests a continual effort to broaden legislative support for the program by blurring its narrow focus on specific targets. Undermining this effort to maintain majority support in Congress was the fact that the national economy improved from the late 1970s to the mid-1980s. Because the market was creating a large number of new jobs without direct government intervention by 1985, there seemed less of a need to stimulate job creation through UDAG. In addition, the perception that UDAG was a big-city rustbelt program was so strong that what support there was from Southern and Western representatives in Congress was tenuous at best.[107]

Montjoy and O'Toole provide insight into the continued attempts to broaden UDAG in their general discussion of targeting of intergovernmental aid. They point out that "explicitly distributive questions invoke the representational roles of legislators. Indeed, the ability to tap the next higher level of government on behalf of district interests has long been a standard campaign theme."[108] It was necessary to convince at least a simple majority in Congress to support UDAG. In order to achieve this level of support, UDAG had to have proponents from all regions of the country. The support would be present only if UDAG benefited cities in all regions on what was perceived to be a fair basis.

However, the need of policies to enjoy more than simple majority support has become accepted in the literature.[109] Copeland and Meier explain:

> The norms of building large and fluid coalitions and of program expansion work to insure that each member has something to take back to the constituents. Congressional coalitions tend to be large—there is no limit on the number of winners. Coalitions that lead to the creation or extension of federal grant programs are large because grants have historically been allocated on a positive sum basis whereby the size of the appropriation is increased to satisfy member demands. . . . [C]oalitions are large because uncertainty in the legislative process encourages building greater-than-minimum winning coalitions.[110]

There is little question that UDAGs were intended to be targeted very specifically in the bill recommended by the Carter administration in 1977. UDAGs were meant to aid low- and moderate-income citizens through job creation and improved housing in the larger, highly distressed rustbelt cities. As the preceding discussion illustrates, it was not possible to forge majority legislative support even in the dark economic days of the late 1970s for a program so narrowly targeted. In order to gain enough supporters to maintain majority support over the eleven-year life of UDAG, adherents agreed to numerous broadening measures.

First, small cities were included and 25 percent of the funds was designated for use in small cities. While many cities under 50,000 population had problems similar to the large distressed cities, many very small eligible communities hardly qualified as urban places and had little in common with America's large cities. HUD had a difficult time in the early years of the program in even generating sufficient applications from small cities to meet the 25 percent mandate.

Second, urban counties were added to the program even though many of them contained the suburbs urban observers claimed contributed to the cities' problems.

Third, cities that were not otherwise eligible were allowed to submit applications if they had pockets of poverty that qualified for aid. This provision likely added more than 200 cities to the list of those eligible for UDAG funding.[111]

Fourth, in developing eligibility criteria for UDAG, HUD's definition of "severely distressed" allowed well over 50 percent of the nation's large cities and over 10,000 small cities to be eligible. The decision to allow such a large number of local governments to apply was a major step in creating broad legislative support. However, it is difficult to understand why a majority of the nation's cities should qualify as "severely distressed."

Fifth, requirements for citizen participation plans and housing assistance plans were eliminated, which made it easier for more communities, especially smaller ones, to compete for funding. The necessary paperwork for an application was reduced considerably. Cities without staff capacity to develop these plans were now more likely to apply, HUD believed.

Sixth, the addition of Labor Surplus Area (LSA) as a seventh criterion under which cities could qualify for funding increased the number of eligible cities.

Seventh, HUD reduced the threshold requirement for qualifying under the pre-1940 housing criterion from 33.98 percent to 21 percent with no explanation in the *Federal Register*. This criterion created the most controversy because it obviously favored the older cities of the rustbelt regions.

Eighth, the two-pot system was installed to allow more funds to go to sunbelt cities as a result of the threats of their congressional delegations to withdraw support for UDAG.

Targeting becomes very difficult to achieve in a program like UDAG where legislative representatives have no incentive to support it if their constituencies are not benefiting directly. In order to maintain legislative support, it becomes necessary to broaden the base of support, which then makes the targeting less effective. It is unlikely that a program perceived to target one or two geographic regions of the country can garner enough congressional support to survive. Either an effort must be made to demonstrate that the program is benefiting other regions, if it truly is, or the program must be broadened to include the other regions. The need to maintain majority legislative support appears to be anathema to targeting of federal urban aid.

CONCLUSION

Lowi's theory of policy types explains much of what took place with UDAG over the life of the program. UDAG was conceived and presented as a redistributive program to assist the nation's most distressed large cities. The numerous efforts to broaden UDAG reflect Lowi's position that Congress prefers to disaggregate policies and programs so that patronage can be spread and conflict can be avoided.[112] In the case of UDAG, if benefits could have been spread geographically until all regions of the country were perceived as benefiting equally, conflict in Congress and among local officials would have been lessened.

The Community Development Block Grant program is an interesting contrast with UDAG in that it has become distributive.[113] It is a formula grant program with wide political support because it "offers advantages for many groups, including those who are politically more influential and for whom, therefore, help is less controversial."[114] UDAG, by legislative design, was not capable of becoming a formula grant program since it required competitive applications. Lowi's claim that Congress is not capable of "complex balancing on a very large scale" and, therefore, not capable of maintaining redistributive programs, appears to be borne out in the case of the UDAG program.[115]

If all the broadening changes had the desired effects, then the UDAG program would have been less targeted to the most distressed and impacted jurisdictions as the program matured. The eight specific measures identified in this chapter taken to broaden UDAG are consistent with the view, derived from Lowi's theory, that redistributive programs will either become distributive or lose political support and languish or die.

UDAG's demise, in hindsight, exemplifies this political dilemma. On one hand, UDAG had to be broadened to maintain political support. On the other hand, when eligibility was broadened, UDAG was criticized for not concentrating on its mandated targets. As Chapter 5 illustrates, these efforts to broaden UDAG's constituency did not materially affect the distribution of the funds. Since the distribution of funds did not change despite these broadening efforts, wider political support could not be maintained.

The next chapter reviews three recurring targeting issues in the UDAG program. Consideration of these three issues will be presented through five major studies completed by government agencies over the life of UDAG. The three issues involve the appropriateness of eligibility criteria, the fairness of the project selection system for funding, and the inability of some cities in need of assistance to participate in the program. The studies are consistent with the findings of this chapter in that they reflect political pressure to move UDAG away from its redistributive purpose and make it more distributive.

NOTES

1. See Edward C. Banfield, *The Unheavenly City Revisited* (Boston: Little, Brown, 1974).

2. John C. Bollens and Henry J. Schmandt, *The Metropolis* (New York: Harper & Row, 1965), 254.

3. Ibid., 255.

4. John R. Gist, "Urban Development Action Grants: Design and Implementation," in *Urban Revitalization*, ed. Donald B. Rosenthal (Beverly Hills: Sage Publications, 1980), 239.

5. Ibid., 240.

6. Ibid.

7. To leverage means to generate investment for a particular purpose from public or private sources through the use of matching funds. Generally, one unit of government will pledge a percentage of the funds needed for a project with the goal of inducing another governmental unit or a private corporation or individual to invest the remainder. For example, UDAG applications were graded on the basis of how many private dollars they generated per UDAG dollar. Each application had to demonstrate that there were at least 2.5 private dollars for every UDAG dollar in the proposed project.

8. Gist, 240.

9. James W. Fossett, *Federal Aid to Big Cities: The Politics of Dependence* (Washington, D.C.: Brookings Institution, 1983), 1–3.

10. Ibid.

11. Ibid.

12. Ingrid W. Reed, "Life and Death of UDAG: An Assessment Based on Eight Projects in Five New Jersey Cities," *Publius* 19 (Summer 1989): 94.

13. Ibid.

14. Congress, House, Committee on Banking, Finance, and Urban Affairs, *Housing and Community Development Act of 1977*, 95th Cong., 1st Sess., 24 February 1977, 21.

15. Ibid., 31–32.

16. Ibid., 33.

17. Ibid.

18. Ibid., 35–49.

19. Ibid., 34.

20. Congress, House, Committee on Banking, Finance, and Urban Affairs, *Housing and Community Development Act of 1977*, 95th Cong., 1st Sess., 28 February 1977, 298.

21. Ibid.

22. Ibid., 486–487.

23. Ibid., 486.

24. Ibid., 487.

25. Ibid., 489.

26. Ibid., 568.

27. Congress, House, Committee on Banking, Finance, and Urban Affairs, *Housing and Community Development Act of 1977*, 95th Cong., 1st Sess., 9 March 1977, 2417.

28. Ibid., 2418.

29. Robert Jay Dilger, *The Sunbelt/Snowbelt Controversy: The War over Federal Funds* (New York: New York University Press, 1982), 39–40.

30. Congress, House, Committee on Banking, Finance, and Urbn Affairs, *Compilation of the Housing and Community Development Act of 1977*, 95th Cong., 1st Sess., October 1977, 259.

31. Ibid.

32. Ibid., 266.

33. Ibid., 354.

34. Ibid.

35. Ibid., 288.

36. Ibid.

37. General Accounting Office, *Insights into Major Urban Development Action Grant Issues* (Washington, D.C.: U.S. General Accounting Office, 1984), 23.

38. P. David Sowell of the Department of Housing and Urban Development, interview by author, 15 August 1990, Washington, D.C.

39. Congress, House, Committee on Banking, Finance, and Urban Affairs, *Housing and Community Development Act of 1977*, 95th Cong., 1st Sess., 1 March 1977, 717.

40. Ibid., 718–720.

41. Ibid., 728.

42. Ibid., 729.

43. Ibid., 716.

44. Ibid.

45. Ibid., 715.

46. Ibid., 719.

47. Ibid., 724.

48. Ibid.

49. Ibid., 725.

50. Ibid.

51. Sowell interview, 15 August 1990.

52. Ibid.

53. Department of Housing and Urban Development, Office of Policy Development and Research, *An Impact Evaluation of the Urban Development Action Grant Program* (Washington, D.C.: U.S. Department of Housing and Urban Development, 1982), 8.

54. Ibid.

55. Ibid.

56. Department of Housing and Urban Development, Office of Evaluation, *Urban Development Action Grant Program: Second Annual Report* (Washington, D.C.: U.S. Department of Housing and Urban Development, 1980), 4.

57. President's Commission on Privatization, *Privatization: Toward More Effective Government* (Washington, D.C.: U.S. Government Printing Office, 1988).

58. General Accounting Office, *The Urban Development Action Grant Application Selection System: Basis, Criticisms, and Alternatives* (Washington, D.C.: U.S. General Accounting Office, 1985), 31.

59. Ibid., 32.

60. Ibid.

61. Ibid., 32–33.

62. Department of Housing and Urban Development, Office of Community Planning and Development, *Annual Report to Congress on Community Development Programs—1989* (Washington, D.C.: U.S. Department of Housing and Urban Development, 1989), 54.

63. Department of Housing and Urban Development, Office of Policy Development and Research, *An Impact Evaluation of the Urban Development Action Grant Program*, Foreword.

64. David A. Stockman, *The Triumph of Politics* (New York: Harper & Row, 1986), 142–143.

65. Department of Housing and Urban Development, Office of the Assistant Secretary for Public Affairs, *New Directions in Housing and Urban Policy: 1981–1989* (Washington, D.C.: U.S. Department of Housing and Urban Development, Office of the Assistant Secretary for Public Affairs, 1989), 52.

66. Ibid.

67. Sowell interview, 15 August 1990.

68. Congress, Senate, Committee on Banking, Housing, and Urban Affairs, *Housing, Community Development, and Mass Transportation Authorizations—1986: Hearing before the Subcommittee on Housing and Urban Affairs*, 99th Cong., 1st Sess., 15 April 1985, 783–785.

69. William Greider, *The Education of David Stockman and Other Americans* (New York: E. P. Dutton, 1981), 12. Also see Reed, 95.

70. Evidence of regional differences over UDAG appears in congressional hearings. For example, see Congress, House, Committee on Government Operations, *Urban Development Action Grant Program*, 96th Cong., 1st Sess., 23 May 1979. Also see *1985 CQ Almanac*, 322; *1986 CQ Almanac*, 161; *1986 CQ Almanac*, 585. *CQ Almanac* is a publication of Congressional Quarterly, Inc., Washington, D.C. For a comprehensive bibliography on the political problems of UDAG, see Lorna Peterson, "The Demise of the Urban Development Action Grant Program: A Bibliography" (Monticello, Ill.: Vance Bibliographies, undated).

71. Sowell interview, 15 August 1990.

72. Department of Housing and Urban Development, Office of Community Planning and Development, *1982 Consolidated Annual Report to Congress on Community Development Programs* (Washington, D.C.: U.S. Department of Housing and Urban Development, 1982), 63.

73. Paul K. Gatons and Michael Brintnall, "Competitive Grants: The UDAG Approach," in *Urban Economic Development*, eds. Richard D. Bingham and John P. Blair (Beverly Hills: Sage Publications, 1984), 126.

74. Ibid.

75. Ibid.

76. Ibid., 127.

77. Ibid.

78. Ibid.

79. Department of Housing and Community Development, Office of Community Planning and Development, *Report to Congress on Community Development Programs—1989*, 57.

80. Department of Housing and Urban Development, Office of the Assistant Secretary for Community Planning and Development, "Community

Development Block Grants; Urban Development Action Grants; Final Rule," *Federal Register* 47-36 (23 February 1982): 7982–7995.

81. Department of Housing and Urban Development, Office of Community Planning and Development, *1982 Consolidated Annual Report to Congress on Community Development Programs*, 63.

82. Department of Housing and Urban Development, Office of the Assistant Secretary for Community Planning and Development, "Community Development Block Grants; Urban Development Action Grants; Final Rule," 7983.

83. Department of Housing and Urban Development, Office of Community Planning and Development, *1982 Consolidated Annual Report to Congress on Community Programs*, 63.

84. Department of Housing and Urban Development, Office of the Assistant Secretary for Community Planning and Development, "Community Development Block Grants; Urban Development Action Grants; Final Rule," 7982.

85. Gatons and Brintnall, 127.

86. Quoted in Gatons and Brintnall, 127.

87. Department of Housing and Urban Development, Office of Community Planning and Development, *1985 Consolidated Annual Report to Congress on Community Development Programs* (Washington, D.C.: U.S. Department of Housing and Urban Development, 1985), 45–46.

88. Department of Housing and Urban Development, Office of the Assistant Secretary for Community Planning and Development, "Urban Development Action Grants Distress Criteria," *Federal Register* 49-17 (25 January 1984): 3074–3076.

89. Ibid.

90. Ibid.

91. Department of Housing and Urban Development, Office of Community Planning and Development, *1986 Consolidated Annual Report to Congress on Community Development Programs* (Washington, D.C.: U.S. Department of Housing and Urban Development, 1986), 65.

92. General Accounting Office, *HUD Review of Urban Development Action Grant to Wilmington, N.C.* (Washington, D.C.: U.S. General Accounting Office, 1986), 1–3.

93. Department of Housing and Urban Development, Office of Community Planning and Development, *1987 Consolidated Annual Report to Congress on Community Development Programs* (Washington, D.C.: U.S. Department of Housing and Urban Development, 1987), 70.

94. Sowell interview, 15 August 1990.

95. Department of Housing and Urban Development, Office of Community Planning and Development, *1988 Consolidated Annual Report to Congress on Community Development Programs* (Washington, D.C.: U.S. Department of Housing and Urban Development, 1988), 46.

96. Department of Housing and Urban Development, Office of Community Planning and Development, *Report to Congress on Community Development*

Programs—1989 (Washington, D.C.: U.S. Department of Housing and Urban Development, 1989), 4.

97. Reed, 106.

98. Ibid.

99. Ibid.

100. Ibid., 93.

101. Ibid., 106.

102. See *Washington Post*, 24 June 1988, A22; and *Wall Street Journal*, 1 August 1988, 14A and 16E.

103. Reed, 107.

104. *Nation's Cities Weekly* (Washington), 27 June 1988, 11.

105. Reed, 107.

106. "Space Station Survives $59.4 Billion HUD Bill," *1988 CQ Almanac*, 728–733.

107. General Accounting Office, *Urban Development Action Grants—Effects of the 1987 Amendments on Project Selection* (Washington D.C.: U.S. General Accounting Office, 1989), 6–7.

108. Robert S. Montjoy and Laurence J. O'Toole, "Policy Instruments and Politics: Multiple Regression and Intergovernmental Aid," *State and Local Government Review* 23-2 (Spring 1991): 52.

109. See Michael J. Rich, "Distributive Politics and the Allocation of Federal Grants," *American Political Science Review* 83-1 (March 1989); and Kenneth A. Shepsle and Barry R. Weingast, "Political Preferences for the Pork Barrel: A Generalization," *American Journal of Political Science* 25 (February 1981).

110. Gary W. Copeland and Kenneth J. Meier, "Pass the Biscuits, Pappy: Congressional Decision Making and Federal Grants," *American Politics Quarterly* 12 (January 1984): 4.

111. Congress, Senate, Committee on Banking, Housing, and Urban Affairs, *Housing, Community Development and Mass Transportation Authorizations—1986: Hearing before the Subcommittee on Housing and Urban Affairs*, 99th Cong., 1st Sess., 15 April 1985, 783.

112. Theodore J. Lowi, "American Business, Public Policy, Case Studies, and Political Theory," *World Politics* XVI-4 (July 1964): 693.

113. Randall B. Ripley and Grace A. Franklin, *Bureaucracy and Policy Implementation* (Homewood, Ill.: Dorsey Press, 1982), 165–167.

114. Ibid., 158.

115. Lowi, 715.

4

Three Targeting Issues Found in Five Government Studies

This chapter reviews efforts by Congress and two government agencies to deal with issues related to targeting in the context of the Urban Development Action Grant Program (UDAG). Five major government studies provide a convenient means to examine these issues and to demonstrate that they were an integral part of the politics of UDAG. The issues identified in this chapter developed from the redistributive nature of the UDAG program. In essence, representatives of areas not targeted by UDAG sought to modify the redistributive policy by making UDAG distributive.

As discussed in Chapter 2, the political tension between targeted and nontargeted cities over UDAG is consistent with public policy theory that suggests redistributive policies are inherently self-destructive. Large, distressed cities of the rustbelt regions (Northeast, North Central, and Mid-Atlantic) were clearly targeted by both legislative and administrative enactments in the UDAG process. Because targeting was such a major element of the Urban Development Action Grant program, UDAG was the subject of an unusual level of scrutiny by Congress and the Reagan administration. Representatives in Congress from areas not as clearly targeted called for close oversight of the program.

Oversight of UDAG was achieved in several ways. First, the Department of Housing and Urban Development (HUD) was required to provide an annual report to Congress to include a listing of the details of every project funded during the prior year.[1] Second, congressional committees instructed the General Accounting Office (GAO) and HUD to report to them on a regular basis on targeting issues members of Congress raised about UDAG. Third, over the life of the program congressional committees held numerous hearings that dealt primarily with UDAG's targeting effectiveness.

The preceding chapters have shown how difficult it is for the federal and state governments to target assistance effectively. Now attention will focus on five major studies completed by government agencies that dealt primarily with questions of UDAG targeting. All five support findings reported in earlier chapters that political issues make it difficult to target federal programs effectively. These studies are as follows: GAO, *Criteria for Participation in the Urban Development Action Grant Program Should Be Refined* (1980); HUD, *An Impact Evaluation of the Urban Development Action Grant Program* (1982); GAO, *Insights into Major Urban Development Action Grant Issues* (1984); GAO, *The Urban Development Action Grant Application Selection System: Basis, Criticisms, and Alternatives* (1985); and GAO, *Urban Development Action Grants—Effects of the 1987 Amendments on Project Selection* (1989).

The fact that Congress demanded these studies supports the hypothesis that political pressures will be exerted on a redistributive program, such as UDAG, to become more distributive. All five studies dealt with issues that reflected political concern over the extent of the redistributive success of UDAG. The concerns expressed in these studies revolved around three recurring issues—reliability and validity of eligibility criteria, reliability and validity of selection criteria, and participation.

The first issue was whether the criteria selected by the Department of Housing and Urban Development were the most appropriate ones to determine which cities and urban counties should be *eligible* to participate in UDAG. The eligibility criteria were foremost in importance to targeting in UDAG because they eliminated from participation in the program one-half of all large cities and urban counties. By not allowing one-half of the large cities into the program, HUD created some degree of resentment, and thereby lost political support, among those constituencies not eligible. Moreover, if those representating noneligible cities believed the criteria used by HUD were unfairly keeping their cities out of UDAG, they worked for one of two ends: (1) to make UDAG distributive so that their cities would be included; or if that failed, (2) to eliminate UDAG by withdrawing their support or even working actively for its termination.

The second issue was whether, after the pool of eligible cities and urban counties was established, the most distressed and impacted jurisdictions within the pool were *selected* to receive UDAG funding. The selection criteria did not become an issue in UDAG until the selection system was instituted in 1983. Prior to that time, all qualifying applications were funded, as Chapter 3 points out. The selection criteria established by HUD were chosen to favor older large cities and urban counties that had little opportunity for physical growth. The selection criteria created political problems for UDAG within the pool of eligible large cities because many of the non-rustbelt cities felt the selection criteria discriminated against them and favored the large cities of the Northeast, Mid-Atlantic, and East North Central regions. Non-rustbelt representatives believed that in order for UDAG to be more distributive among all eligible cities, the selection criteria needed to be changed to eliminate regional bias. Representatives of large cities in the eligible pool were likely to withdraw their political support for a program that did not give their cities a fair chance to compete for UDAG funding.

The third issue Congress wanted examined centered on the failure to participate in UDAG of many eligible cities and urban counties that did have serious problems of distress and impaction. The participation issue differs from the issues of eligibility and selection in that HUD targeted the UDAG program to these eligible cities but they failed to participate. Many of these cities not only were eligible to participate but also were favored in the selection system because of their physical and economic problems. Efforts were made by Congress through the availability of technical assistance grants, and by HUD through various outreach programs, to include cities that were targeted but not participating in the UDAG program. These efforts reflected a desire to sharpen UDAG's targeting effectiveness, especially among small cities. The cities' failure to participate illustrates a weakness in a targeted program that is dependent on the initiative and ability of local units of government to apply for the available funds.

These questions had important practical effects because political support for UDAG was closely tied to its ability to respond to legislative mandates. On one hand, the intent of the legislation creating UDAG was to target funding to the most needy cities. On the other hand, if members of Congress believed HUD was discriminating against their constituents, either in eligibility or selection, they were unlikely to support UDAG's continued existence. This dilemma resulted in close scrutiny by Congress and the scrutiny itself tended to encourage HUD to broaden the UDAG eligibility and selection criteria and standards.

The five GAO and HUD studies that examined these issues reflect the practical concerns of members of Congress over targeting of UDAG.

CRITERIA FOR PARTICIPATION IN THE URBAN DEVELOPMENT ACTION GRANT PROGRAM SHOULD BE REFINED (GAO 1980)

The basic question facing HUD after enactment of UDAG was how to determine which cities were eligible to participate. It is extremely important to note that HUD controlled the criteria for eligibility, and therefore could determine how many cities and urban counties were defined as "severely distressed." The formula developed by HUD resulted eventually in slightly more than one-half of the large cities and urban counties and over 10,000 small cities being eligible to apply for UDAG assistance.[2]

In 1979, a little over one year after the first program year, the House Subcommittee on Intergovernmental Relations and Human Resources requested the GAO to study the UDAG eligibility criteria. Some committee members were concerned that the eligibility criteria selected and implemented were biased against newer, particularly Southern and Western, local jurisdictions.[3] GAO restricted its study to the eligibility criteria used for large cities and urban counties.[4]

Three criteria, which HUD later identified as "impaction," were listed in Section 119(e)(1) of the 1977 Act:

> [T]he Secretary shall establish selection criteria for grants under this section which must include (A) as the primary criterion, the comparative degree of economic distress among applicants, as measured (in the case of metropolitan city or urban county) by the differences in the extent of growth lag, the extent of poverty, and the adjusted age of housing in the metropolitan city or urban county.[5]

While the House-Senate Conference Report on UDAG did not assign weights to the three impaction variables, HUD did in its regulations after the program began. (See *Code of Federal Regulations*, Section 570.459(c)(1).) In addition, HUD selected three "distress" variables that were not identified in the legislation: per capita income growth, unemployment rate, and employment growth.

In summary, for large cities and urban counties, six criteria were chosen to determine eligibility. These criteria were age of housing, poverty, population growth lag, per capita income, unemployment, and job lag.[6] HUD chose the six criteria for large cities and urban counties from among the nine it originally considered "because they were either direct measures or proxies for the eligibility factors discussed in the authorizing legislation."[7]

For a city or county to be eligible, it had to be ranked in the lower one-half of all jurisdictions in at least three of the six categories.[8] By 1979, 52 percent or 333 of the nation's potentially eligible 646 large cities and urban counties, according to the 1970 Census, qualified as "severely distressed" under the HUD formula.[9] By the end of the program, 53 percent (444 of 840) of the potentially eligible large cities and urban counties, according to the 1980 Census, were eligible.

Difficulty of Specifying Criteria

GAO's 1980 analysis of the eligibility criteria illustrates the difficulty of identifying factors to use in targeting federal aid. The selection of criteria has both practical and political problems. The practical problems involve the reliability of the data as well as their validity in terms of accurately measuring the targeted problem. The political problem is that one group or jurisdiction will be favored over another because of the choice of one factor over another.

In examining the nine potential impaction and distress criteria, GAO appeared to agree with the HUD reasons for rejection of three of the measures.[10] The following three criteria were not selected by HUD:

1. *Housing abandonment*, measured by delinquent property taxes, was not used because it was based on a city's practice for collecting delinquent property taxes. A city with a strict policy of foreclosing on delinquent taxpayers would have a considerably higher abandonment rate than would a lenient city.

2. *Local tax base* was rejected by HUD following comments by the Treasury Department and the Office of Management and Budget that cities have considerable leeway in assessing property, which rendered tax base not a comparable measure nationwide.

3. *Condition of housing* was also rejected because cities use different standards in determining housing conditions.[11]

GAO was also critical of the six criteria that were chosen. GAO concluded in its report to Congress:

The six criteria HUD selected to measure urban distress and eligibility for the UDAG program are based on data that is old and of varying degrees of reliability and that was not specifically designed for HUD's use. Thus, the criteria cannot always be relied on to capture current distress problems. The data, however, generally is the most current available.[12]

Specifically, GAO criticized each of the eligibility criteria measurements as follows:

Population Growth Lag—This was based on the difference in population in each jurisdiction between the 1960 Census data and the 1976 Census estimate. By 1979, the 1960 data were nearly twenty years old and the reliability of the 1976 data was questionable since Census estimate was a new calculation for the Bureau of the Census. HUD's goal was to identify "cities which have lost population over an extended period."[13] GAO believed that a shorter time frame (1970–1976) would be more valid for identifying cities with current problems. Furthermore, the 1960 Census data were not adjusted to reflect annexations by cities.[14] This factor, which in the technical language of measurement reflects problems of instrumentation and content validity, worked against Southern and Western cities that had more open space in which to grow.

Age of Housing—The amount of pre-1940 housing compared with total houses in a city comprised the age of housing criterion and was based on 1970 Census data. GAO concluded: "This criterion does not take into account condition of housing, however, and as a result may not be the most accurate discriminator of distress."[15] Much older housing was better constructed and better maintained than some newer housing that was in poorer condition, had low value, and generated little taxes.[16] HUD's criterion, however, overlooked these facts, GAO found.

GAO recommended that HUD use age of rental housing as the measure for this criterion. It based its recommendation on a 1979 HUD study that concluded "that housing problems are pinpointed more accurately when pre-1940 housing is associated more directly with rental housing and low income categories of residents."[17] The study showed

> that pre-1940 rental housing in central cities had a 10.3 percent incidence of poor housing compared to only 1.5 percent poor housing for owner-occupied pre-1940 housing. Additionally, pre-1940 rental housing had a 9.7 percent incidence of poor neighborhoods, compared to only a 3.9 percent incidence in owner-occupied pre-1940 housing. These results provide a strong indication that there is a significant difference between pre-1940 rental housing and pre-1940 owner-occupied housing.[18]

The HUD study also showed that post-1940 rental housing was in poorer condition than was pre-1940 owner-occupied housing.

Per Capita Income—GAO pointed out two problems with the data used to determine per capita income. First, it was based on a 20 percent sample, which, "due to sampling variability, . . . may differ from the results of a complete count, particularly in small cities."[19] Second, the income data used by HUD were five to ten years old. The possibility that current conditions were not represented was present. However, GAO decided that HUD was using the best available measurement despite its shortcomings.

Poverty—GAO cited three "significant problems" with the poverty criterion. First, the data were based on a 20 percent sampling method used in the 1970 Census and in the 1976 estimated population. GAO concluded that both sets of data exhibited serious reliability problems.[20] Second, poverty level is determined as a national statistic that resulted in understating poverty in cities with high costs of living and overstating it in cities with low costs of living. Third, this criterion was based on the poverty level in 1970, by then nearly ten years old.

While not recommending an alternative, GAO was especially concerned about the reliability of the poverty measurement:

> These problems for the poverty criterion are compounded by the fact that HUD weights poverty more heavily than the other five criteria in determining UDAG eligibility by allowing cities to receive two eligibility points if poverty is 1½ times the median and to lose one point if poverty is less than half the median.[21]

Job Lag—Besides the data being eight to thirteen years old, GAO recognized that manufacturing and retail employment usually did not represent the entire economy.[22] With the growth in service industries in many cities, relying strictly on manufacturing and retail jobs distorted the data on the local job market. GAO suggested that retail sales may be a better indicator than job lag to determine distress because manufacturing "employees can be shifted to other sectors of the economy through productivity increases but at the same time a city's economic condition could be stable or improving."[23]

Unemployment—While national unemployment data are reliable, local unemployment rates are not reliable because of the "composite technique" used by the Bureau of Labor Statistics.[24] Local unemployment rates are estimates based on statewide data generated from unemployment compensation records. The estimates are not broken down for smaller jurisdictions, but the estimated percentages for the larger areas in which they are contained are simply assigned to them.

GAO concluded that "the six eligibility criteria HUD uses to make eligibility determinations for the UDAG program are based on unreliable and old data."[25] Three of the criteria (population growth lag, age of housing, and job lag) were based on questionable assumptions for the reasons cited above.

GAO also performed a correlation analysis of the six criteria "because a high degree of either positive or negative correlation may have the effect of double-counting distress for those criteria which are highly correlated." GAO did not distinguish between the three factors of distress and the three factors of impaction. Instead, correlation analysis was used to test among all six criteria. The analysis showed age of housing had a −0.77 correlation with population growth lag and a −0.63 correlation with job lag. Job lag and population growth lag had a correlation of 0.66 while all others were less than 0.5.[26] Those variables that had a positive relationship fluctuate together in the same direction consistently. For example, when job lag increased, population growth lag also increased in the GAO analysis. Those variables that are negatively related moved in opposite directions when the independent variable changed. When age of housing increased, the population growth lag criterion decreased.

GAO concluded that those criteria that showed correlations above 0.5 (positive or negative) may have had the effect of double-counting some impaction and distress elements. Two of the three variables with high correlations were impaction criteria—age of housing and population growth lag. GAO suggested that other "distress indicators," such as population density, crime rate, education levels, dependency, budget deficits, and female heads of households, be tested to find the ones with correlation coefficients closer to zero so that redundancy would not occur.[27] Table 4-1 presents the results of GAO's correlation analysis of all six eligibility criteria.

Severity of Distress

Another major GAO criticism of the HUD process of determining eligibility was that it was not sensitive to the differences in severity of distress among cities since a city was either eligible or it was not eligible. GAO noted: "HUD's system is not sensitive to severity of distress on the individual criteria, except poverty. For example, a city with 14 percent unemployment is economically worse off than a city with 6 percent unemployment, yet both cities would meet HUD's current standard."[28]

HUD's system overlooked cities that were severely distressed on two criteria and, therefore, did not qualify even though another city might barely qualify under three of the six criteria. GAO reported finding one city with more than an 8 percent unemployment rate and 15 percent poverty rate but that failed to meet a third criterion to qualify for UDAG.[29] If the data were not reliable, a small error in accuracy could determine whether a city was eligible or not.

GAO's Alternate Methods

To address the problem of judging severity of distress, GAO suggested alternate methods of determining eligibility. One method was to assign cities to one of four quartiles with those in the top quartile receiving three points, the next highest two points, the third highest one point, and the lowest quartile no points. Rather than meeting three of six criteria, a city would have to accumulate enough points to be eligible.[30]

TABLE 4-1

Spearman Rank Order Correlation Coefficient Matrix
for the Six Eligibility Criteria*

Eligibility Criteria	Percent in Poverty	Age of Housing	Population Growth Lag	Per Capita Income Growth Lag	Unemployment Rate	Job Lag
Percent in Poverty	1	0.39	−0.41	−0.42	0.46	−0.19
Age of Housing	0.39	1	−0.77	−0.30	0.24	−0.63
Population Growth Lag	−0.41	−0.77	1	0.26	−0.25	0.66
Per Capita Income Growth Lag	−0.42	−0.30	0.26	1	−0.47	0.21
Unemployment Rate	0.46	0.24	−0.25	−0.47	1	−0.25
Job Lag	−0.19	−0.63	0.66	0.21	−0.25	1

*Source is GAO 1980 study, p. 26.

A second proposed method was to use standardized scores for each of the six criteria based on distress indexes for all 646 large cities and urban counties potentially eligible in 1979 for UDAG. Of that total, GAO determined that between 48 and 56 cities would have their eligibility changed.[31] Using this "more sensitive" method as compared with HUD's method, GAO concluded that

> most eligibility changes would occur for those cities which are barely eligible or ineligible. This indicates that while HUD's present system does a good job of classifying cities which are clearly eligible or ineligible, it does not discriminate well among those cities which are close to the margin.[32]

Effect of the Study

This study addressed the first issue of targeting identified in the introduction to this chapter—that it was difficult to develop appropriate criteria to determine eligibility for the UDAG program. GAO's criticism reflects problems of reliability, validity, and redundancy in the six measures of distress and impaction chosen by HUD.

It is important to note how much discretion HUD had in choosing not only some of the measures to use but also the weight given to them in determining eligibility. For example, HUD could have reduced the number of eligible cities and urban counties just by requiring four of the six thresholds established for the various measures to be met. Or, the thresholds for eligibility for each measure could have been adjusted upward, limiting the number of eligible cities. Of course, the numbers of eligible jurisdictions could have been increased by taking the opposite action. Questions of eligibility, then, were primarily left in the hands of HUD.

This study had no apparent immediate impact on UDAG. There was no evidence of any of the GAO recommendations in the "Clarifications and Changes to Urban Development Action Grant Rules" published in the *Federal Register* two months after the study was presented.[33] None of the six criteria for eligibility was changed except the term "population lag/decline" was altered to read "population growth lag/decline" even though the definition of the term remained the same.

AN IMPACT EVALUATION OF THE URBAN DEVELOPMENT ACTION GRANT PROGRAM (HUD 1982)

The second major question concerning the UDAG program was whether the grant selection criteria targeted the funding to the most distressed and impacted cities among those eligible to participate. Once cities were declared eligible to apply for funding, HUD had to develop a system to select the projects proposed from among eligible cities that most clearly reflected the congressional mandate on how and where to use the funds. The intent of Congress was clear that the UDAG funds were to be used in the cities determined to be worst off under the broad guidelines of the legislation. HUD decided that the same criteria used for eligibility were to be employed to determine which projects were to be selected for funding. As a practical matter, HUD had sufficient funds to approve all qualified applications through 1983. A HUD study completed in 1982 addressed matters relevant to the issue of selection, and also to the issue of participation, as explained below.

HUD 1982 Study Results

Early in the Reagan administration, Secretary Samuel Pierce instructed Assistant Secretary E. S. Savas to study the UDAG program in detail and report his recommendations to him. Savas and his research team selected a representative sample of eighty projects in seventy cities. They inspected many of the sites and conducted in-depth interviews with many of the key players on the public and private sides of each transaction. In addition, Savas formed a "blue ribbon" panel of experts in real estate and finance to examine the elements of each UDAG.[34]

The Savas team sought to determine whether the cities with the greatest need for economic development were receiving the funds. If they were not receiving the funds, the research team wanted to determine why they were not participating in UDAG. Participation, or lack of participation, is the third major targeting issue identified in this chapter and was of primary concern to the Savas team. The UDAG program's express purpose was to assist cities that met the criteria of economic distress and impaction. However, even though a city was severely distressed, it did not automatically receive UDAG funding. Cities still had to have the staff capacity as well as the initiative to submit competitive applications.

Among large cities, Savas found that over 60 percent of the UDAG awards were made to the most severely distressed cities.[35] Savas concluded that this targeting of distressed cities was "due primarily to the large number of UDAG applications submitted by the most distressed group of cities rather than any competitive advantage in the application process. The less distressed large cities, in effect, select themselves out of the UDAG competition to a certain extent by applying less often."[36]

Administrative Impact on Targeting

One of the research questions in "An Impact Evaluation of the Urban Development Action Grant Program" (HUD 1982 Study) dealt with both eligibility and selection criteria: "Are UDAG funds distributed among cities in a way that is consistent with the purposes of the program?"[37] Assistant Secretary Savas concisely summarized the choices HUD had to consider with the UDAG program:

> Within terms set by the Congress, UDAG can be either a targeted program for the most highly distressed cities or a program that ignores variations of distress among eligible cities. If the program is to be targeted, awards or funds should go disproportionately to cities with the greatest relative distress. On the other hand, if the goal is to encourage as much participation as possible among all eligible cities, targeting of program awards is not as important. Therefore, depending on which goal is preferred, different options are suggested.[38]

If UDAG was to be targeted to the most distressed cities, the Savas team suggested three options to achieve this goal: (1) change the selection formula to place greater weight on distress and impaction criteria; (2) eliminate from the eligibility list many of the less distressed and less impacted cities by increasing the number of distress and impaction thresholds; and (3) increase the technical assistance to the most distressed and most impacted cities to improve their chances of funding.[39] On the other hand, if the goal was to increase the base of participation by all eligible cities, the HUD staff could place a limit on the number of grants or the amount of money any one city could receive. In addition, technical assistance could be offered to all eligible cities with few or no prior awards regardless of level of distress.[40]

The choices posed by the HUD 1982 study again demonstrate that HUD had considerable leeway to shape the targeting of the UDAG program. The first set of options was aimed at improving the targeting effectiveness of the program. It was difficult for some to understand why over half of America's large cities were considered to be in the category of "severely distressed." If targeting was to be improved either option 1 or option 2 would have lessened the number of eligible cities by making it more difficult to qualify for the program. These options stressed the social goals of UDAG while the alternative of widening the base of participation would have worked to broaden UDAG's political base.

Conclusion

The HUD 1982 study dealt with all three major issues in targeting discussed in this chapter. Its importance to targeting is that the three issues of eligibility criteria, selection criteria, and participation were clearly identified as central to the political acceptability and success of the

UDAG program. It presented options to the secretary of HUD on the questions of program eligibility, on the selection of projects on the basis of distress and impaction versus merits, and of assisting cities that lacked technical capability to participate in UDAG. The choices made by the HUD secretary on these issues had a clear impact on the targeting effectiveness of UDAG. While the HUD 1982 study appeared to be the primary factor in securing Secretary Pierce's support for UDAG, it did not result in a dramatic change in policy direction for UDAG. Many of the changes undertaken to broaden UDAG in subsequent years were identified in the HUD 1982 study but there is no evidence to suggest that they were made on the basis of this study.

INSIGHTS INTO MAJOR URBAN DEVELOPMENT ACTION GRANT ISSUES (GAO 1984)

One of the greatest targeting challenges for the UDAG program was presented by small cities. Their lack of participation, especially in the earlier years of the program, provides the principal context in which the third issue of targeting examined in this chapter arises: despite serious problems of distress and impaction, why did many eligible cities not participate in UDAG? Three major reasons for nonparticipation became evident—lack of knowledge, lack of staff capacity, and lack of capital from the private sector.

UDAG was conceived by the Carter administration as a program to assist large urban areas that had severe problems as reflected in the criteria of distress and impaction. However, as Chapter 3 points out, small cities were included in the UDAG program by Congress before final passage in 1977. Their inclusion was important in securing sufficient legislative support for UDAG but was contrary to the program intent of large city aid proposed by Secretary Harris.

Since HUD could not allocate unused small city funds to metropolitan city/urban county grants, it wrestled with the problem of generating quality applications from small cities. Congress mandated that 25 percent of the funds was to be dedicated to projects in small cities, which generally meant communities under 50,000 population in non-Standard Metropolitan Statistical Areas. By the end of FY 1982, $142 million of the $216 million set-aside for small cities was unobligated. Nearly half of the total was carried over from prior years and one-half was the amount appropriated for FY 1982.[41]

In its 1984 report entitled "Insights into Major Urban Development Action Grant Issues," the General Accounting Office, in preparation for Congress's consideration of UDAG reauthorization in 1985, sought answers to the questions: "Why have many potentially eligible, very distressed small cities not applied for UDAG funds and why have some applicant small cities not been successful?"[42] Congress, in recognition that many small cities needed assistance to participate in the UDAG program, had authorized up to $2.5 million for technical assistance for small cities in the Housing and Urban-Rural Recovery Act of 1983 for FY 1984, FY 1985, and FY 1986.[43] By October 1982, however, less than 8 percent of the 10,161 potentially eligible small cities had applied for UDAG funding while only 4 percent had been successful.[44]

Methodology

In an effort to understand why so many small cities were not participating through applications in the UDAG program, GAO interviewed key officials in the most heavily distressed cities in the following categories:

1. 25,000–49,000 population—4 nonapplicant cities and 2 unsuccessful applicant cities.

2. 2500–24,999 population—123 nonapplicant cities and 28 unsuccessful applicant cities.

3. 2500 and less population—426 nonapplicant cities and 3 unsuccessful applicant cities.[45]

All of these cities had impaction percentiles of 25 or less on a rating scale of 1 to 100. The lower the rating, the more distressed was the city based on "the age of the city's housing stock, the degree of its poverty, and the lag in its population growth."[46] In addition, GAO interviewed UDAG's seven senior development officers who were responsible for the UDAG application process.[47]

Study Findings

GAO found that participation by small cities was strongly associated with city size. As population decreased, the percentage of cities participating and succeeding in the UDAG program declined. Over 68 percent of the cities over 40,000 population had applied and all of them had been successful, even though the number of cities (13 of 19) was not large. About one-half of all cities over 10,000 population had applied for a UDAG with one-third of them receiving at least one.[48] However, cities in the 10,000–50,000 population range represented only about 5 percent of all eligible small cities. The great bulk of eligible small cities (9,625 of 10,161) had populations of less than 10,000. A further breakdown by GAO found that 8,077 of the eligible small cities had populations under 2,500 while half of that number had populations under 500 residents.[49]

The success rate, that is, the percentage of cities that received funding, for all small cities was only 4.2 percent by October 1982. While a third of the eligible small cities over 10,000 population had received a UDAG, only 2.6 percent under 10,000 and only 0.2 percent of the under-500 population cities had been successful. GAO noted that the success rate for small cities that were applicants was 53.9 percent overall with even the under-2,500 population cities receiving funding 37.4 percent of the time.[50] This meant that only a small percentage of eligible small cities were applying but, among those that did apply, over one-half were successful in receiving UDAG funds.

An important finding by GAO was that 75 percent of the mayors and development directors interviewed were not even aware of the UDAG program. Again, the results showed that the degree of awareness declined as population decreased. One hundred percent of the cities interviewed in the 25,000–49,999 population group had either "great" or "moderate" awareness of the program. Only 17 percent of the smallest cities had any awareness of UDAG.[51] The UDAG senior development directors agreed that lack of knowledge of UDAG among small cities was a serious problem. However, they believed HUD's outreach efforts were frustrated to a large degree by the small cities' narrow communication networks and lack of professional staff.[52]

GAO found that of the 150 cities that were aware of UDAG, one-half had contacted HUD about the UDAG program. Almost all were pleased with HUD's explanation of the program but none had applied. In response to GAO's questioning, many cited their lack of staff capabilities as the reason for not applying.[53]

Obstacles to Participation

GAO described the task faced by small cities in submitting a competitive UDAG application:

A good deal of planning is needed to structure a UDAG application. An eligible city—large or small—must present HUD with a specific project that is well developed. The city must describe the project's nature, scope, and benefits. The city must also demonstrate that the project would not be economically feasible without UDAG funding by providing detailed construction estimates and cash flow projections and analyses. In addition, the city must provide evidence of financial capacity and firm commitment from the developer, the lending institution, and other involved parties.[54]

Approximately one-third of the cities indicated they lacked the capacity for project planning and development.[55] It is likely that many more were similarly incapable of producing a competitive UDAG application but did not realize it.

Other cities responded that they had not filed a UDAG application because private sector participants were not available to them.[56] Developers and lending institutions were critical of the UDAG process because projects were funded only with firm private sector commitments to invest money to create jobs and new taxes. Over half of the small cities believed developers were not interested. GAO could have also pointed out that in the smallest cities there is little development activity anyway and most of it is by local, relatively unsophisticated developers. A high percentage (over 75%) of nonapplicant small cities had "great" or "very great" difficulty in securing private sector commitments.[57]

Lack of private financial commitments was the primary cause highly distressed small cities did not receive UDAGs even when they did apply. Thirty-two of the forty-three applications filed by highly distressed cities failed because applicants had problems with financing. Interestingly, eight of the forty-three rejected projects were built anyway.[58] However, seven of those were reduced in scope and five received other government aid, either from state or federal sources. Only one of the eight proceeded as proposed with the developer's funds.[59]

GAO's Recommendation

Because HUD was not meeting its 25 percent mandate for small city funding by 1983, GAO concluded that HUD needed to do a better job of reaching distressed small communities through the following actions:

- Develop a plan aimed at helping severely distressed small cities participate in the UDAG program by (1) identifying highly distressed, potentially eligible small cities that have not applied for, or received, funding; and, (2) establishing goals and criteria for selecting small cities to receive technical assistance to help them participate in the UDAG program.

- Develop comprehensive UDAG information materials to help educate small cities and the private sector about the program.

- Develop and test a streamlined application form for use by small cities.[60]

HUD's Response

HUD responded that it had already developed an outreach program that was resulting in many more small city applications by 1983. The July 1983 funding round included announcements for eighty-four projects, the largest number of small city applications ever approved in one round.[61]

As far as GAO's recommendation to single out highly distressed cities for technical assistance, HUD responded:

"This is not a proper role for HUD. The UDAG program is by law a national competition. We cannot favor one city over another. It is a local decision to apply for UDAG assistance. It is the obligation of this Office to promote the program and provide program information. As the data indicate, the largest number of small cities is under 2,500 in population, including many severely distressed cities. It is likely that development opportunities may not be available in these cities. We cannot and should not try to create development opportunities where they do not exist. We only have a limited staff and limited technical resources available to assist cities with all phases of the UDAG process. We have made the decision to concentrate our scant resources on viable UDAG deals." (quotation marks in the original)[62]

HUD also disagreed with GAO's recommendation to develop a stream-lined application form for small cities because the "information called for is the minimum amount needed by HUD to make funding decisions."[63] HUD did agree to develop more informational materials for small cities and the private sector.

The attitude of the UDAG staff was reflective of its view of its roles as "underwriters" and "deal makers."[64] Staff members believed the limited UDAG funds should be invested in the cities that were most capable of managing the UDAG process. Furthermore, they felt there were limited opportunities for UDAG gap financing in many small cities, so staff effort should be expended where the greatest likelihood of successful ventures existed. In short, cities had to have the initiative to pursue UDAG funding if they wanted to benefit from it.

HUD's response to the GAO recommendations is interesting in relation to the question of targeting, and particularly the participation issue. While HUD's eligibility and selection criteria were clearly chosen to target distressed and impacted cities, HUD believed its obligation to target was limited to those areas. It was up to distressed and impacted cities to respond on their own to the opportunities presented by the eligibility and selection systems. Given the results of GAO's small city survey as reported here, it appears that this dependence on the initiative and ability of eligible local governments to participate in UDAG lessened the ability of HUD to target effectively.

THE URBAN DEVELOPMENT ACTION GRANT APPLICATION SELECTION SYSTEM: BASIS, CRITICISMS, AND ALTERNATIVES (GAO 1985)

An important change for the UDAG program took place in early FY 1984 when a selection formula was instituted. Until that time, HUD had sufficient funds to award UDAGs to all qualifying applicants. Congress had reduced the appropriation for UDAG for FY 1982 from $675 million the previous year to $440 million. At the same time, cities were submitting more qualifying applications as their level of expertise in the program increased.[65]

The selection formula exacerbated the regional differences over UDAG and focused congressional attention on the issue of selection: were the most distressed and impacted jurisdictions selected to receive UDAG funding? Congressional concerns over this issue led to a major GAO study of the UDAG selection system in 1985. This section reports on that study as it relates to the issue of the distribution of UDAG funds.

In 1983, Secretary Samuel R. Pierce created a HUD task force to develop a competitive selection formula.[66] The task force consisted of representatives from various HUD offices, such as General Counsel, Policy Development and Research, and Community Planning and Development. The selection formula devised by the task force had a 100-point maximum score consisting of 40 points for impaction, 30 points for distress, and 30 points for merits of the project.[67] The composite scores of proposed projects were compared with each other and all were ranked from highest to lowest. Applications were approved from the list in order until the available funds for each competitive round were exhausted.

Effects on UDAG

Creation of the selection formula had two major effects on the UDAG program. First, the selection formula with its emphasis on distress and impaction, especially the latter, was apparently constructed to favor the older cities and urban counties of the Northeast and Midwest. Seventy of the 100 possible points were based on distress and impaction factors. HUD appeared to make it intentionally difficult for newer cities with relatively high distress and impaction ratings to compete with older cities with low ratings even if the merits of their projects were superior.[68]

Second, the formula process had the effect of removing discretion from the UDAG staff in selecting the best projects.[69] The intent of the formula, to a large degree, was to predetermine the winners of each round. Even if the quality of a proposed project from a most distressed and impacted city was not as meritorious as other applications, chances for funding were generally excellent.

HUD's official position on the selection formula is summarized in its 1985 report to Congress: "The formula strongly reflects existing statutory and regulatory requirements concerning the factors used to define the selection criteria and the relative weight given to each criterion."[70]

GAO reported to Congress that "because of existing statutory criteria, HUD believes that the UDAG criteria for application selection should be dealt with by the Congress."[71]

One of the primary goals of the selection system was to assure targeting of UDAG funds on the bases of impaction and distress. With its heavy emphasis (70 points) on the physical and economic conditions of large cities, the selection system made it clear that UDAG funds were to be targeted to those cities with the worst conditions. The selection system, simply by the way it was constituted, reflected HUD's commitment to the targeting goals of UDAG. In terms of the focus of this book, the selection system can be seen as a strategy for preserving the redistributive intent of the program in the face of the distributive pressures on the UDAG program. Some have argued that the formula hurt the UDAG program politically in that it appeared to make funding for Southern and Western cities even more difficult. In addition, the flexibility for a highly qualified staff to make judgments on which projects were best was eliminated.[72]

Criticism of Pre-1940 Housing Criterion

A major criticism in Congress of the selection formula was the weight given to pre-1940 housing, which accounted for one-half of the impaction score. HUD selection formula task force members admitted to the GAO that there might be a "strong case for de-emphasizing pre-1940 housing" since the focus of the UDAG program had become economic development.[73] However, they defended the use of the pre-1940 housing criterion on the grounds that it correlated strongly "with other measures of physical distress for metropolitan communities."[74] Furthermore, they felt cities with considerable growth and newer homes were unlikely to rate highly under any criteria used to judge distress or impaction.

GAO reported that HUD task force members did believe that one refinement to the pre-1940 housing measure would have more accurately reflected the distress of a community. Instead of using simply the percentage of pre-1940 housing, the HUD task force members recommended using the number of poverty-level families in pre-1940 housing.[75] They recognized that much older housing has been well maintained while some more recently constructed housing may be in poor condition. Nonetheless, HUD concluded that it did not have the authority to make this change because the use of pre-1940 housing as a criterion was specifically called for in the UDAG legislation.

Alternate Scoring Weights

The HUD task force considered the effect that deemphasizing pre-1940 housing would have on the impaction scores of cities in the different regions of the country. If the three criteria making up the impaction score (pre-1940 housing, poverty, and population growth lag) were given equal weight, cities in Florida, Georgia, North Carolina, Puerto Rico, South Carolina, Texas, and Virginia would have benefited.[76] Cities in Illinois, Indiana, Iowa, Massachusetts, Minnesota, New York, Pennsylvania, and Wisconsin would have suffered.[77]

If poverty were emphasized by assigning it 50 points, pre-1940 housing 25 points, and population growth lag 25 points, an even greater effect was created on impaction rankings. Obviously states with high poverty populations would have benefited the most. HUD identified them as Alabama, California, Florida, North Carolina, South Carolina, Puerto Rico, Texas, and Virginia. On the other hand, Illinois, Indiana, Iowa, Massachusetts, New York, Ohio, Pennsylvania, and Wisconsin would have been adversely affected.[78]

HUD made the conscious decision to assign most weight to the impaction criterion of pre-1940 housing that favored the older cities of the Northeast, Mid-Atlantic, and North Central regions. Clearly, acceptance of either of the other alternatives the task force considered would have benefited the Southern states primarily. This choice in weighting the formula toward the older cities of the three "rustbelt" regions demonstrates again the important role administrative agencies, such as HUD in this case, play in targeting.

Impact of the Selection Formula

In its 1985 annual report to Congress, HUD claimed that the impact of implementing the selection formula was felt almost immediately. In FY 1984, HUD reported 67 percent of all UDAG funds were given to the one-third most impacted large cities and urban counties.[79] By comparison, for the FY 1978 to 1983 time period, 61 percent of the UDAG dollars had been granted to the one-third most impacted large cities and urban counties. Under the formula, only 8 percent of UDAG funds went to the one-third least impacted cities and counties. Prior to the formula, 14 percent of the money went to the least impacted communities.[80]

These shifts are not especially large, contrary to the impression HUD conveyed to Congress, because in both cases there was a difference of only 6 percent from the previous year. Variations in funding of this magnitude were not uncommon from one year to the next. Furthermore, there was no evidence to prove that these changes were due to the selection formula.

The distribution of UDAG dollars among small cities also was affected by the formula, according to HUD. In FY 1984, the one-third most impacted small cities received 47 percent of the funds compared with 37 percent in the period prior to FY 1984. The formula did not help the one-third moderately impacted small cities in FY 1984. The percentage of dollars they received dropped from 27 to 22. The least impacted small cities were funded at the same rate (36%) as they had been in the earlier years.[81] Again, these changes are not especially impressive, especially when one realizes that the one-third least impacted cities still received over one-third of the funds.

HUD's motive in claiming greater success at redistribution is not clear. On one hand, HUD officials may have been responding to criticism of not targeting successfully enough by representatives of highly distressed areas. Conversely, HUD may have been overtly rejecting distributive pressure. A third possibility is that UDAG program leaders were both responding to redistributive pressure and rejecting distributive pressure.

Reporting Inconsistencies

HUD's claim that the "introduction of the project selection formula in FY 1984" caused these funding changes was not based on any supporting evidence. Moreover, in its 1986 annual report, HUD, without explanation, increased its report of the percentage of funds going to the one-third most impacted large cities for FY 1984 from 67 percent to 75 percent and claimed 89 percent of the funds went to the most impacted jurisdictions in 1985. The 1986 report also lowered the percentage of funds for the one-third most impacted small cities for 1984 from 47 percent to 42 percent but claimed 56 percent of the funds in 1985 went to the one-third most impacted small cities.[82] The changes in the numbers from one annual report to the next for the same prior reporting period were not explained and create questions about their reliability.

Locality Points

In this same 1985 study, GAO also attempted to determine how *combined* impaction and distress ratings related to funded and unfunded applications in the first year of the selection formula—FY 1984. The prior analysis considered only the relationship between impaction criteria and funding levels for eligible cities. Distress criteria were not included in

HUD's reports to Congress, nor did they appear in the earlier GAO analysis.

In each funding round after the selection formula was instituted, HUD's standard process was to rank all projects by number of earned points, with the ones with the highest number of point totals funded first. Projects were funded in order on the list until all available funds were expended. GAO combined the distress points (30 points) and impaction points (40 points), which represented 70 of the possible 100, and labeled them "locality points."[83] In doing the analysis in this manner, GAO attempted to show Congress the impact of both distress and impaction criteria in UDAG funding decisions.

The 1985 GAO report to Congress stated that 41 percent of the projects funded for three funding rounds in 1984 had locality points of 50 or greater while no unfunded projects had scores that high.[84] Nearly three-fourths of the funded applications had locality scores over 40 while only 2 percent of the unfunded projects rated that high in locality points. GAO concluded that there was a positive relationship between higher locality points and project funding—projects with higher locality points were more likely to be funded than those with lower locality points.

Project Merits

GAO also examined each of the 1984 projects on the basis of their merits. The quality of the project appeared to have much less effect on funding decisions than did the locality factors of distress and impaction.[85] Twenty-six percent or 37 of the 141 unfunded applications had over 20 project merit points out of a possible 30 (see Table 3-1). Applications that received over 20 project merit points were generally considered sound business propositions by the UDAG staff. Presumably, these applications were from cities that had low locality (distress and impaction) points and, therefore, did not have high enough total points to qualify for funding. Conversely, 28 of the 231 projects (12%) actually funded had merit scores below ten, which were projects the UDAG staff had judged not to be sound.[86] These applications came from jurisdictions with very high impaction and distress ratings, and were funded even though they were financially questionable or risky projects.

The GAO 1985 study demonstrated that the selection formula favored large cities with high distress and impaction scores. Furthermore, 26 percent of the applications with more than 20 project merit points were not funded because they were from cities that did not score well on the distress and impaction criteria. The selection system apparently was achieving HUD's targeting goals for UDAG, according to the GAO. When HUD had sufficient funds to approve all qualifying applications prior to the selection system, there was no political issue involving selection criteria: only issues of eligibility criteria and participation arose. The effects of the GAO 1985 study were to make clear to representatives of cities not favored by the selection formula that the redistributive nature of the UDAG program must be changed to benefit their constituencies.

GAO Alternatives to Selection System

Congressional hearings to consider criticisms of the selection formula were held in early 1985. Representative Henry B. Gonzalez (D-TX), chairman of the Subcommittee on Housing and Community Development, had requested GAO to report to the Subcommittee on potential alternatives to the existing selection formula.[87] GAO identified for the Subcommittee two alternatives to the HUD system. Both alternatives increased project merit points to 50 while reducing the value of impaction and distress factors. The first alternative reduced impaction and distress to 25 points each while alternative 2 lowered impaction to 10 points and raised distress to 40 points. The intent of the reduction of impaction points in alternative 2 was primarily to neutralize the pre-1940 housing impact on funding decisions.[88]

If alternative 1 had been in effect during the 1984 funding rounds, 15 unfunded projects would have received UDAG awards while 12 funded projects would not have been successful. Over $10 million of the total $18.4 million that would have been reallocated under alternative 1 would have gone to Southern and Western cities, primarily in California and Texas. On the losing side would have been cities primarily in Connecticut, Massachusetts, New Hampshire, and New York.[89]

Alternative 2 produced a greater change in the applications that would have been funded. More than twice as much money was involved (over $40 million). Thirty-three projects would have received UDAGs that had not received them and twenty-five would have lost funding.[90] The primary losers would have been cities in New Hampshire and New York, although all the losing cities except Louisville, Kentucky, and Monroe, Louisiana, were Northeastern or Midwestern cities.[91] By contrast, twenty-six of the thirty-three cities that would have gained funding under alternative 2 were in the South Atlantic, Pacific, or Caribbean regions.[92]

While the alternate formulae would have helped the non-rustbelt regions, the size of the changes needs to be placed in perspective. During the three 1984 funding rounds studied by GAO, grants worth $380 million were awarded to cities. Alternative 1 would have altered only 4.8 percent of the funds. Alternative 2 would have reallocated 10.6 percent of the UDAG funds.[93]

It is apparent that other factors accounted for the allocation of a majority of the funds since nearly 90 percent of the projects funded would have remained the same even with project merits raised to 50 points and impaction reduced to 10 points. Little attention was ever given to this finding even when the formula was later changed by Congress. This finding is important because so much effort was expended by opponents of UDAG as a redistributive program to change the formula. GAO's analysis indicated that a changed formula would produce little difference in the cities that received UDAGs.

However, one possible explanation for the relatively minor changes that the GAO alternatives produced merits discussion. It is likely that cities favored by the HUD selection formula more actively sought UDAG funding because their chances of success were high. Cities not favored were likely to seek other ways than UDAG of funding their projects or not develop them at all. When GAO analysts applied their alternative formulae retrospectively to the 1984 funding rounds, they could not have accounted for this factor. If the formula had actually been changed and then studied, greater changes might have been found to have taken place. HUD's policy position on targeting was clearly reflected in the selection formula that encouraged those cities favored by it to participate.

GAO advised Congress that the advantage to changing the selection formula would be to fund applications that produced the most economic benefits.[94] More jobs would be created and more private funds would be leveraged with the UDAG dollars under either of the alternatives. No immediate action was taken by Congress to change the formula following the presentation of the GAO report to the House Subcommittee on Housing and Community Development.

Summary and Conclusion

The important points raised by the GAO 1985 study as they relate to targeting are the following:

1. Implementation of the selection formula in FY 1984 created a third issue of selection criteria; this was not present in the earlier years of the UDAG program because all qualifying applications were funded.

2. The formula was designed to emphasize the redistributive nature of UDAG by targeting the large cities with the most severe problems of distress and impaction.

3. Fairness of the selection formula became an issue in Congress for representatives whose constituent cities were placed at a competitive disadvantage.

4. Regional variations became apparent with Southern and Western cities calling for HUD to make UDAG more distributive by deem-phasizing the factors of impaction and distress. The impaction criterion of pre-1940 housing drew especially heavy criticism.

5. HUD reported to Congress in its 1985 annual report that the selection formula improved the targeting effectiveness of UDAG. However, the actual shifts in funding the first year under the selection system were not large and may have been due to other explanations.

6. GAO combined impaction and distress points into a "locality score" and concluded that there was a positive relationship between higher locality scores and project funding. In other words, the selection formula was effective in targeting the more heavily impacted and distressed cities.

7. GAO presented two alternative formulae to Congress and both would have shifted more funding to the non-rustbelt regions. However, neither alternative would have changed more than 10 percent of the funding.

The selection system was consistent with the redistributive nature of UDAG: it gave heavy weight to the factors of distress and impaction. Prior to the selection system implementation, HUD had sufficient funds to award UDAGs to all eligible cities that submitted qualifying applications. The concern in Congress, prior to the selection system, was over eligibility issues, not project selection issues. Now, with fewer funds and more sophisticated local government applicants, it was necessary for HUD to select from among qualifying applications for the first time. After the selection system was instituted, it was not enough for a city simply to appear on HUD's eligibility list. For the first time, many marginally eligible cities were at a competitive disadvantage under the selection system despite the merits of their applications. This situation brought UDAG under close scrutiny by members of Congress whose interests were not in UDAG successfully targeting the nation's most distressed and impacted jurisdictions but in receiving part of the funding for cities in their districts.

URBAN DEVELOPMENT ACTION GRANTS—EFFECTS OF THE 1987 AMENDMENTS ON PROJECT SELECTION (GAO 1989)

Congressional criticism of UDAG from many Southern and Western members became sufficient by 1987 to result in changes in the project selection formula.[95] Amendments through the Housing and Community

Development Act of 1987 were specifically aimed at achieving a more equitable geographical distribution of UDAG funds through a lessening of the importance of impaction and distress factors. In order to achieve this, the 1987 law "placed greater emphasis on project factors and less on community factors."[96] Congress required 35 percent of all UDAG funds to be awarded based strictly on the merits of the proposed projects with one or two bonus points for cities without a grant in the prior one- to two-year period.[97]

HUD developed a two-pot system to implement this legislative mandate. Using its traditional criteria, HUD approved proposed projects until 65 percent of the available funds were committed. After that, applications with the most project points plus bonus points were funded. Distress and impaction factors were not considered in the second pot during each funding round.[98]

In addition, the law also gave less weight to the impaction factors of pre-1940 housing, poverty, and population lag, and more weight to the distress factors of per capita income, unemployment, and job lag/decline. This change was apparently made to favor newer growing communities in the South and West that had serious unemployment problems but did not have older housing or declining populations. A $10 million cap on funds a city could receive in any one round was also implemented.[99]

GAO Findings

Included in the legislation was a requirement for GAO to report to Congress how these changes "affected the allocation of UDAG funds."[100]

> Specifically, GAO was directed to analyze the effect of the changes during fiscal year 1988, on (1) the distribution of grant funds among regions of the United States, (2) the targeting of grant funds to cities and urban counties having the highest degree of economic distress, (3) the number and types of projects receiving grants, (4) the per-capita funding levels of each city, urban county, or identifiable community receiving grants, and (5) the stimulation of maximum economic development activity.[101]

In 1989 GAO analyzed the two large city and two small city rounds that had been held since the 1987 amendments. In these rounds HUD awarded 59 grants in response to 132 qualifying large city applications, and 57 grants in response to 89 eligible small city applications.[102] GAO concluded that the 1987 amendments had the intended effects.[103] The East North Central and the Mid-Atlantic regions received less funding under the new system than they would have under the old system even though those two regions still accounted for 72 percent of all large city funds.

Under the old system, they would have received over 80 percent of the allocations. Six of the other 10 regions slightly increased their shares of the funds.[104] A similar pattern was evident for small city funding.[105] Since some change did take place each year in funding by region, the percentage changes noted by GAO do not seem unusual enough for GAO to have declared that the formula changes had the desired effect.

GAO also scored the applications under the old and new systems to analyze the impact of the formula change. The most distressed large cities lost nineteen projects under the new system that would have been funded under the old system. The projects not funded represented over $26 million that went to less distressed cities elsewhere. The most distressed small cities lost ten projects and $7.4 million as a result of the new formula.[106] If GAO's findings were correct, they indicated a weakening of UDAG's effectiveness as a targeted program, which was the purpose of the 1987 amendments.[107]

Total allocations for the two large city rounds in 1987 were $146 million while $43.6 million was granted for the two small city rounds. Eighteen percent of the funding of large city grants was altered as to recipient cities by the new formula while 17 percent of the small city funds was reallocated under the new formula.[108] It is noteworthy that well over 80 percent of the funding was not affected by the formula change.

HUD's Position

In an apparent contradiction to the conclusions of the GAO study on the effect of the 1987 amendments, HUD told Congress in its 1989 Report:

> In FY 1988 and FY 1989, 84 percent of the money going to large cities went to the one-third most impacted cities, compared to 63 percent from FY 1978 to FY 1987. Only six percent of the grants went to the one-third least impacted communities, compared to 14 percent from FY 1978 to FY 1987.[109]

In addition, HUD reported that funding to the one-third most impacted small cities increased from 42 percent for FY 1978 through FY 1988 to 56 percent for FY 1989.[110] An apparent contradiction arises because HUD told Congress that an even higher percentage of the UDAG funds went to the most impacted cities after 1987 while GAO indicated that the UDAG funds were spread more widely. In effect, HUD reported that it was even more effectively targeting UDAG despite the change in formula.

HUD did not mention the 1987 amendments in its last UDAG report to Congress but one may conclude from the statement quoted above that HUD officials believed the 1987 amendments did not have the effect reported by GAO and intended by Congress.

Conclusion

This study illustrates the continuing congressional concern over the redistributive nature of UDAG. Changing the formula to make UDAG more distributive was an obvious attempt to secure broader political support. The results of the two-pot system in achieving broader distribution, and thus a lessening of targeting effectiveness, are not clear. GAO claimed the changes in the selection system had the desired effects while HUD's reports to Congress indicate that UDAG was even more effectively targeted after the two-pot system was implemented.

DISCUSSION OF METHODOLOGICAL ISSUES

The various studies on the eligibility and selection criteria raise several methodological questions that relate to the three issues discussed in this chapter (see Table 4-2). First, were the six, and later seven, criteria used by HUD the best available? The evidence is certainly not clear. The 1979 GAO study was critical of the age and reliability of the data but concluded that they were probably the best available for the criteria actually chosen by HUD. However, GAO recommended using the percentage of pre-1940 rental housing as the measure to replace pre-1940 housing. Even though GAO's recommendation was based on a 1979 HUD study, it was not accepted by HUD.

Second, were the measures selected by HUD redundant? The GAO concluded that age of housing was strongly correlated with population growth lag and with job lag. The effect of this finding is that age of housing, population growth lag, and job lag were all measuring the same problem, and thus, "double-counting" the same phenomenon. Based on the GAO 1980 study, it is difficult to know whose political interests were advanced because GAO did not distinguish between impaction and distress criteria. GAO's criticism was primarily methodological in suggesting that less strongly correlated variables be chosen.

Third, and most important, did the eligibility and selection measures really make a difference anyway? Of course they did for the one-half of the large cities and urban counties that were not even eligible to apply. For those jurisdictions that were eligible, the evidence is not clear how important they were in deciding which ones received funding.

GAO's 1980 study, which was critical of the HUD measures, concluded that the alternatives it studied would have "only changed the

TABLE 4-2

Matrix of Three Major Targeting Issues
in Five Government Studies

Studies	Eligibility Criteria	Selection Criteria	Participation
GAO 1980	–Problems of validity, reliability, and redundancy. –System not sensitive for severity of distress. –Alternative methods proposed.		
HUD 1982		–HUD had choices to make UDAG distributive or redistributive. –Choices made by HUD secretary reflect administrative role in targeting.	–Most distressed cities participate more often and receive more funds.
GAO 1984			–Lack of participation due to three reasons: • lack of knowledge • lack of staff capacity • lack of capital from private sector –City size related to participation.
GAO 1985		–Selection system formula stressed impaction and distress factors. –Formula made regional differences apparent. –Alternate systems would not have made major changes in funding patterns. –"Locality points" correlate positively with funding.	
GAO 1989		–"Two-pot" system evaluated. –GAO concluded "two-pot" system worked; HUD concluded it did not have desired effect.	

eligibility of cities close to the margin." In project selection, the 1985 and 1989 GAO studies indicated the same result, that formula changes would have affected the marginally qualifying projects but not the bulk of those funded. The HUD 1982 study found that the most important variable was the large number of applications submitted by most distressed cities "rather than any competitive advantage in the application process." This conclusion was made prior to the institution of the selection formula but the distribution of funds did not change greatly over the life of the program.

When the HUD task force on the selection formula tested altering the weight given to different criteria, cities in the South and West benefited the most. However, under the scenario making the most change, only approximately 10 percent of the funds would have been reassigned.

After the selection process was actually changed by Congress to the two-pot system in 1987, little perceptible change was made in funding patterns. GAO claimed the new system was successful in responding to congressional intent even though the amount of funds going to rustbelt cities decreased by only 8 percent. Furthermore, no evidence was given to show that the 8 percent change was due to the new formula. It could just as well have been explained by numerous other variables. In contrast, and very strikingly, HUD concluded that even a greater amount of the funds following the formula change went to the most impacted cities, contrary to the intent of the Congress! Apparently, Congress was not convinced that the two-pot system was effective or politically desirable, for it eliminated UDAG funding after the first year under the new system.[111]

DISCUSSION AND CONCLUSION

The government's own studies of UDAG reveal the difficulty of targeting intergovernmental aid. Three recurring issues were seen in the five studies prepared by two separate governmental agencies:

1. It was very difficult to identify and implement valid and reliable criteria for eligibility that could withstand practical and political challenges. Despite the legislative mandate to target the "most severely distressed" cities, HUD had great difficulty in choosing criteria that were clearly recognized as accomplishing that mandate. A major part of the problem was recognized by GAO: data that precisely measure the problems to be targeted by UDAG were simply not available. The measures used by HUD were not developed for UDAG but were simply the best available data.

2. The selection formula had to favor either cities that were most impacted or distressed or those that submitted the best applications

regardless of impaction and distress ratings. As the HUD 1982 study pointed out, HUD had latitude in emphasizing either the targeting goals of UDAG or the economic development goals of job and tax creation. The choice of the targeting goals was consistent with the legislative mandate of UDAG, HUD believed. However, it did create political problems for UDAG in those cities not favored by the formula. The dilemma faced by HUD was that it would have had political problems through the choice of either goal.

3. Targeting is especially difficult to achieve when its success is dependent on the initiative and ability of local governments to participate. In the case of UDAG, Congress and HUD made special efforts to encourage cities with serious problems of impaction and distress to participate. However, in a competitive project grant program dependent on grant applications, the granting agency's role is limited to a large degree, as HUD pointed out in its response to the GAO 1984 study.

Relatively early in the program, as reflected in the GAO 1980 study and the HUD 1982 study, the issue of eligibility fairness was of concern to members of Congress whose constituents were not benefiting from UDAG because their cities were not eligible under HUD's formula. Later, after the selection system was instituted, the concern of Congress turned to the issue of selection fairness. The GAO 1985 and GAO 1989 studies responded to congressional questions about the tendency of the HUD selection system to favor older cities in the Northeast, Mid-Atlantic, and East North Central regions. The GAO 1984 study dealt primarily with the third issue identified in this chapter: why did so many small cities fail to participate in UDAG despite serious problems of distress and impaction?

The significance of these studies for targeting is that they illustrate the practical and political problems redistributive government programs face. Practical problems include identifying criteria for eligibility and selection that actually accomplish the targeting goals of the program. Political problems revolve around maintaining majority support in the legislature by balancing the targeting (redistributive) purposes of the program with the representational pressures (distributive) brought by legislators and their constituents who are not benefiting from the program.

Certainly, HUD responded to political pressures to broaden the UDAG program, as shown in Chapter 3. It also appeared to try to conform to congressional mandates, found in the enabling legislation, to target the "most severely distressed cities." In this political context, a further point to be drawn from these studies is the importance of administrative agencies in determining policy regarding targeting. Throughout the life of UDAG, HUD determined which cities would be eligible for the program, which cities' applications would be favored by the selection system, and whether cities would be given technical assistance necessary to apply for funding. In sum, this redistributive program required the exercise of a great deal of bureaucratic discretion.

Based on the ideas of Theodore Lowi, it appears that redistributive policies are inherently self-destructive unless there exists some overriding support that compensates for their redistributive character. If this theory is correct, then the difficulty in maintaining targeted, redistributive programs is immense. Either the program must become distributive or it will be eliminated. The government's own studies of UDAG support this theory. Regardless of the amount of discretion available to bureaucrats, UDAG foundered on political opposition. The studies that Congress commissioned, as reviewed here, suggest that the reasons for UDAG's demise are deeply seated in the competitive nature of political interests. The lesson for planners of future programs of this type is to anticipate that political problems, including both the pressure for greater distributiveness and the tension between targeting need and targeting merit, will be compounded by problems of empirical method and administrative limitations.

NOTES

1. *Housing and Community Development Act of 1977*, 91, sec. 119(a) (1977), 1125.

2. General Accounting Office, *Criteria for Participation in the Urban Development Action Grant Program Should Be Refined* (Washington, D.C.: U.S. General Accounting Office, 1980), i.

3. Ibid., cover letter to the Honorable L. H. Fountain, Chairman of House Subcommittee on Intergovernmental Relations and Human Resources from Elmer B. Staats, Comptroller General.

4. Ibid., 2.

5. The Institute for Professional and Executive Development, Inc., *UDAG Update* (Washington, D.C.: Institute for Professional and Executive Development, 1984), I-6.

6. Ibid., i.

7. Ibid.

8. Ibid.

9. General Accounting Office, 1980, 4.

10. Ibid., 4.

11. Ibid.

12. Ibid., 8.

13. Ibid., 9.

14. Ibid.

15. Ibid., 10.

16. Ibid.

17. Ibid., 11.

18. Ibid.

19. Ibid., 12.

20. Ibid., 13.

21. Ibid., 14.

22. Ibid.

23. Ibid., 15.

24. Ibid., 16.

25. Ibid., 18.

26. Ibid., 17.

27. Ibid.

28. Ibid., 20.

29. Ibid., 21.

30. Ibid., 23.

31. Ibid., 24.

32. Ibid., 25.

33. Department of Housing and Urban Development, "Community Development Block Grants; Clarification and Changes to Urban Development Action Grant Rules," *Federal Register* 45-93 (12 May 1980): 31,262.

34. Department of Housing and Urban Development, Office of Policy Development and Research, *An Impact Evaluation of the Urban Development Action Grant Program* (Washington, D.C.: U.S. Department of Housing and Urban Development, 1982), ii, 9–15.

35. Ibid., v.

36. Ibid.

37. Ibid., 166.

38. Ibid., 177.

39. Ibid., 178–179.

40. Ibid., 179–180.

41. General Accounting Office, *Insights into Major Urban Development Action Grant Issues* (Washington, D.C.: U.S. General Accounting Office, 1984), 20.

42. Ibid., 3.

43. Ibid., 20.

44. Ibid.

45. Ibid., 25.

46. Ibid.

47. Ibid., 26.

48. Ibid., 21.

49. Ibid., 22.

50. Ibid.

51. Ibid.

52. Ibid.

53. Ibid., 27–28.

54. Ibid., 27.

55. Ibid., 28.

56. Ibid., 28–30.

57. Ibid., 30.

58. Ibid., 32.

59. Ibid.

60. Ibid., 36–37.

61. Ibid., 37.

62. Ibid., 38.

63. Ibid., 38–39.

64. P. David Sowell, Department of Housing and Urban Development, interview by author, 15 August 1990, Washington, D.C.

65. General Accounting Office, *The Urban Development Action Grant Application Selection System: Basis, Criticisms, and Alternatives* (Washington, D.C.: U.S. General Accounting Office, 1985), 4–5.

66. Ibid., Appendix I, 5.

67. Ibid.

68. Ibid., 7.

69. Sowell interview, 15 August 1990.

70. General Accounting Office, 1985, 46.

71. Ibid., Appendix II, 9.

72. Sowell interview.

73. General Accounting Office, 1985, 8.

74. Ibid.

75. Ibid.

76. Ibid., 9.

77. Ibid.

78. Ibid.

79. Department of Housing and Urban Development, *1985 Consolidated Annual Report to Congress on Community Development Programs* (Washington, D.C.: U.S. Department of Housing and Urban Development, 1985), 51.

80. Ibid.

81. Ibid., 52.

82. Department of Housing and Urban Development, *1986 Consolidated Annual Report to Congress on Community Development Programs* (Washington, D.C.: U.S. Department of Housing and Urban Development, 1986), 70.

83. General Accounting Office, 1985, 16–17.

84. Ibid., 17.

85. Ibid., 18.

86. Ibid.

87. Ibid., 1.

88. Ibid., 22.

89. Ibid., 23.

90. Ibid., 24–25.

91. Cities in the following states were losers under alternative 2: Connecticut, Delaware, Illinois, Kentucky, Louisiana, Massachusetts, Maryland, Maine, Minnesota, Missouri, New Hampshire, New York, and Vermont.

92. Cities in the following states were winners under alternative 2: Alabama, California, Florida, Georgia, Illinois, Michigan, North Carolina, Ohio, Pennsylvania, Puerto Rico, Texas, and Virgin Islands.

93. General Accounting Office, 1985, 24–25.

94. Ibid., 26.

95. General Accounting Office, *Urban Development Action Grants—Effects of the 1987 Amendments on Project Selection* (Washington, D.C.: U.S. General Accounting Office, 1989), 2.

96. Ibid.

97. Ibid., 3.

98. Ibid.

99. Ibid., 1.

100. Ibid.

101. Ibid., 3.

102. Ibid.

103. Ibid., 4.

104. Ibid.

105. Ibid., 17–23.

106. Ibid.

107. Ibid., 6.

108. Ibid.

109. Ibid.

110. Congress, Senate, Committee on Banking, Housing, and Urban Affairs, *Housing, Community Development, and Mass Transportation Authorizations—1986: Hearing before the Subcommittee on Housing and Urban Affairs*, 99th Cong., 1st Sess., 15 April 1985, 783–785.

111. Ingrid W. Reed, "Life and Death of UDAG: An Assessment Based on Eight Projects in Five New Jersey Cities," *Publius* 19 (Summer 1989): 107.

5

Who Got What from UDAG?

The Urban Development Action Grant (UDAG) program was intended to be a targeted effort to assist America's most needy cities in developing new jobs and taxes through private sector investment. It was redistributive in that only distressed and impacted cities qualified for the program. Funds were to be redistributed from wealthier communities to those less well off through federal taxation and appropriation processes.

The congressional mandate to spend UDAG appropriations in the most "severely distressed cities" was clear. Section 119(e)(1) of the Housing and Community Development Act of 1977 authorized the secretary of Housing and Urban Development to establish eligibility and selection criteria based on the "comparative degree of physical and economic distress among the applicants." Furthermore, the secretary was to identify factors relevant in the assessment of "the comparative degree of physical and economic deterioration in cities and urban counties."

Public policy theory can be read to assert that a redistributive program is inherently self-destructive unless there is some overriding support for it that compensates for its redistributive nature. The literatures on policy arenas and targeting suggest that redistributive, targeted programs will be under significant political pressure to become more distributive, that is, to serve broader, nontargeted clienteles.[1] Therefore, if a redistributive program does not have support that compensates for its redistributive nature, it is likely either to become distributive or be eliminated.

The first question addressed by this study was whether UDAG was subject to political pressure to become more distributive. There is considerable evidence that it was under constant pressure to broaden its base of participation over its eleven-year life, as Chapters 3 and 4 demonstrate. Because of these pressures to become more distributive, UDAG would seem to fit the pattern for other targeted federal programs, such as the War on Poverty, the Economic Development Administration, the Comprehensive Employment and Training Act, and the Community Development Block Grant. All started as targeted programs but became more distributive over time through the political process.[2]

The evidence of pressure to broaden UDAG raises the second question that has guided this study. What was the agency's response? Although the legislative mandate to target the most severely distressed cities was clear, leaders in HUD knew that UDAG would not survive unless it had a national constituency.[3] Chapter 3 identified eight measures designed to broaden UDAG's appeal. While some were legislative initiatives, others, such as the addition of the seventh eligibility criterion of labor surplus area or the lowering of the threshold of the pre-1940 housing criterion, were administrative. Were these steps to broaden the allocation of funds or were they cosmetic gestures to placate critics? In this chapter we examine both the decision processes used by HUD and their distributional outcomes in order to reach some judgment about the agency's strategy.

In Chapter 2 we suggested several possible strategies for an agency under pressure to modify its direction. It could stick to its interpretation of its formal mandate and thereby risk losing the support necessary to continue funding. In this case such a strategy would concentrate benefits on those cities that most clearly met the objective measures of both distress and impaction established by HUD in response to the original statute. We call this the *program strategy*.

A second strategy would be responsiveness to current political demands through broadening the allocation as much as possible. An observable consequence of this strategy would be a change in the pattern of allocations so that funds were distributed more equally among units of government or even individual recipients. Because most of the debate about distributional equity for the UDAG program was framed in terms of cities and regions we base our analysis on governmental units rather than population. We call this the *distributive strategy*.

Yet the strategy of broadening the base as much as possible would not produce universal political support, for the original beneficiaries would then lose significantly. A third alternative would, therefore, be a *mixed strategy*. HUD could have yielded to logrolling pressures in part, while still targeting part of its funds, in hopes of keeping the program alive. Such behavior could result from a sophisticated strategy to balance competing external forces, from simple reactions to different pressures at different times, or from political processes among different actors within the agency.[4]

Under any of these strategies—program, distributive, or mixed—the agency would have to defend its actions in terms of its formal statutes, possibly reinterpreting mandates to support actions that it wanted or needed to take as other agencies have done on occasion.[5] Inferring a strategy from the record is, therefore, difficult. In the following section we describe HUD's decision processes, and then we try to measure their outcomes in terms of both programmatic and political criteria.

TARGETING IN PRACTICE

In the early years of the program, before 1983, sufficient funds were available to award grants to all eligible applicants. So, as far as need was concerned, applicants had simply to clear the threshold of meeting three of the six need criteria: *pre-1940 housing, poverty, population growth, per capita income, lag in job growth*, and *unemployment*. (See Figure 5-1 for detailed measurements of the six factors plus a seventh that was added later.) A project that cleared this threshold and was satisfactory on other grounds, such as private participation, would be funded.

During this time, several studies produced mixed conclusions on the targeting success of UDAG allocations. All of these studies examined cities over 50,000 population, leaving out the issue of targeting in the approximately 10,000 small cities that were potentially eligible. Cho and Puryear concluded that HUD had failed to target cities based upon their "degree of distress" although they agreed that UDAG was "highly targeted on distressed cities in the absolute" because only one-half of all cities were defined as eligible to apply for funding.[6] Gist and Hill reported that no distress measures were related to the awarding of grants.[7] Conversely, Webman found that the most distressed quartile of cities received nearly four times the number of grants received by the least distressed quartile.[8] Rich also concluded that need was a significant predictor of UDAG awards but found in a multivariate analysis that it was less important than private funds or population. All of these studies focused on the early years of the program.

By 1984 applications that met the eligibility criteria had exceeded the available funding. At this point HUD began using a rating scale to distinguish among those applicants that cleared the first threshold. The rating scale, which is described in Chapter 4, was based upon measures of **impaction** (40%), **distress** (30%), and the **merit** of the proposed project (30%). The labels assigned to the first two components of the rating scale are confusing because "distress" was used in the statute to describe the general needs of the cities to be aided by the program. But for the purpose of ranking eligible cities, the terms would have specific meanings.

FIGURE 5-1

Data Factors for Distress and Impaction Calculations*

IMPACTION—40 points

Population Growth (20%)

> The percentage of population growth for each place over the period 1960–1984 derived from Census Bureau data qualification. Those places with a percent of 25.3 or less received one point for this factor.** Some places may not have data for this factor, since 1960 population estimates are not available for places that incorporated after 1980. Those places receive no point for this factor.

Poverty (30%)

> The percentage of persons who lived under the poverty line during 1979 for the 1980 Census. Those communities with 12.3 percent or more receive one point for this factor. Those places that are less than 6.2 percent lose a qualification point.

Pre-1940 Housing (50%)

> The percentage of the housing units that were built prior to 1940 according to the 1980 Census. A place receives one qualification point for this factor if it is 20.2 percent or more.

DISTRESS—30 points

Per Capita Income (33 1/3%)

> The per capita income growth for each place over the period 1969 to 1983 derived from Census Bureau data. A place receives one point for this factor if its per capita income growth is $6,203 or less.

Job Lag (33 1/3%)

> The percentage of job lag, where available, is a measure of job creation over the period 1977 to 1982 derived from the Census Bureau's Censuses of Retail Trade and Manufactures.
>
> The percentage job lag for most places is based on combined retail-manufacturing job data. The threshold for receiving a point on this factor for the combined job lag data is 3.3 percent or less. For some communities, only retail data were completely available. For those places a percentage job lag for the retail sector was computed and an *R* placed next to the percentages. The retail job lag threshold is 8.5 percent or less. For a few other places, only manufacturing data were completely available. For those places a percent job lag for the manufacturing sector was computed and an *M* placed next to the percentage. The manufacturing job lag threshold is 0.0 percent or less. A place receives one point for the applicable job lag factor if its job lag percentage is less than or equal to the respective threshold.

Unemployment (33 1/3%)

> The annual average unemployment rate for 1986 based on data from the Bureau of Labor Statistics (BLS). A place receives one point for this factor if its unemployment rate was at least 6.5 percent.

Labor Surplus Area

> The percent of the average monthly labor force for the years 1984–1985 that was unemployed. Places with a two-year average unemployment rate of at least 9.0 percent were designated effective April 1, 1987, to be part of a Labor Surplus Area by the Employment Training Administration (ETA). Those places receive one point for this factor.

*Source is HUD memo dated October 20, 1987, from John Nagoski, Director, Data Systems and Statistics Division, CAS to Mike McMahon, Director, Program Policy and Support Divisions, CCUP.
** In order to be eligible to apply for UDAGs, a city or urban county had to qualify under at least three of the seven criteria listed in this figure.

Impaction was a function of *pre-1940 housing* (weighted at .5), *poverty* (weighted at .3), and *population growth* (weighted at .2). **Distress** was a function of *per capita income*, the *lag in job growth*, and *unemployment*, all weighted equally. As described in Chapters 3 and 4, the determination of **merit** involved issues not directly related to city need.

The choice of these measures reflects discretion on the part of HUD. While the elements of the impaction scale are specified in the enabling statute, the distress scale represents HUD's interpretation of its mandate to include measures of economic distress. Furthermore, HUD chose the relative weights of impaction, distress, and project merit. However, having gone through rule making as required by the Administrative Procedures Act and having established these measures and weights as the interpretation of its mandate, HUD could not very easily change them.

The way in which the scale was used is also significant. At each funding round the secretary would be presented with a list of eligible proposals ranked according to the composite scale of impaction, distress, and merit. Each proposal was reduced to a single line of computer printout, which included the amount of funds requested and the cumulative request summed from the top of the list. The cumulative request represented the dollar consequences of funding that proposal and all higher-ranked proposals. Thus, if the highest-ranked proposal requested $1 million and the second proposal requested $3 million, the cumulative request shown with the second proposal would be $4 million. In principle, the secretary could simply take the amount of money available and draw a line under the last proposal for which the cumulative request did not exceed the funds available.

In practice, the procedure was not automatic for two reasons. First, the secretary could decide how far to go down the list in a particular funding round. Of course, the total amount committed could not exceed the amount available in any budgetary cycle, but there were usually several funding rounds per year. So the secretary could exercise discretion, particularly in the early rounds of each year.

Table 5-1 shows the results of all funding rounds between the adoption of the rating system in 1984 and the adoption of the two-pot system after the January 1988 round. We have omitted the "pockets of poverty" applications because their need criteria were calculated on a different basis. This omission here should not change the results of the analysis very much; in only three funding rounds did the total of project funding under this category edge over $10,000,000. Reading down the column labeled FUNDED reveals that HUD went much further down the funding list in some years than in others. Similarly, the percentage of total fiscal year funding that HUD allocated varied substantially by round. This would appear to be a significant exercise of discretion.

TABLE 5-1

Analysis of Selected Funding Rounds

	Applications		$ Award (× 1000)	% of FY Funding	Rating Points	
	Number	Funded			All Applications	Minimum Funded
March 84	133	100.0%	$216,402	53.3	13.5–80.7	13.5
June 84	84	48.8%	$62,956	15.5	14.5–84.1	52.4
Sept 84	151	45.7%	$126,300	31.1	14.6–90.7	50.4
Total	368		$405,658			
Jan 85	142	25.4%	$77,866	29.1	11.3–84.1	61.3
May 85	138	58.7%	$136,742	51.0	11.5–91.9	49.1
Sept 85	74	54.1%	$53,401	19.9	11.7–87.6	47.6
Total	354		$268,009			
Jan 86	91	60.4%	$87,500	33.3	11.1–91.9	43.4
June 86	50	100.0%	$86,924	33.1	24.1–79.0	24.1
Sept 86	55	58.2%	$88,289	33.6	23.0–83.9	56.3
Total	196		$262,713			
Jan 87	56	100.0%	$106,593	46.1	16.4–79.1	16.4
Sept 87	57	93.0%	$124,399	53.9	26.0–79.1	29.3
Total	113		$230,992			
Jan 88	58	34.5%	$49,662		26.8–80.1	62.7

Pockets of Poverty Omitted

It is, of course, possible that the variations in funding were due to variations in the quality of applications. The last two columns in Table 5-1 address this possibility. They report on the ranking points that HUD staff had assigned to all the proposals in that funding round based upon the criteria of impaction, distress, and merit. Under the heading ALL APPLICATIONS we can see that the range in points assigned to the applications submitted was quite broad for each round. The adjacent column gives the cutoff point for that round, the score beneath which no application was funded. The scores cluster in two distinct groups: one, a range from 47.6 to 62.7 when HUD funded 60 percent or less of the available applications, and the other, a range from 13.5 to 29.3 when HUD funded 93 percent or more of the eligible applications. The explanation that HUD varied the funding by round so as to select only the best projects fails.

The ability to decide how many projects to fund in a particular round appears to have been a significant source of discretion. While we have referred to HUD as if it were a single actor, it is important to identify where this discretion lay. The staff prepared the rankings based upon the criteria described above. According to testimony of a former HUD official, the decision of how many applications to fund in a given round was made in the office of the HUD secretary after the ranked list was prepared. In this way the system could have been manipulated to reach favored projects.[9] If it were, other low-scoring projects in the same round would have been beneficiaries.

Yet the secretary's discretion was not unlimited. He respected the rank ordering of projects provided by the formula and he could not exceed the total amount of funds available in any fiscal year. The need to come out even at the end of the fiscal year was the apparent cause of another exercise in discretion. Normally, if a project ranked high enough, it would be funded regardless of the size of the request, but a large project near the bottom of the funding list at the end of the fiscal year was in jeopardy. For example, in September 1987, HUD had nearly $130 million left to allocate for that fiscal year. Working down the list it had approved forty-nine projects for a total of nearly $124 million. The next proposal in rank order was a request for $7.5 million, which exceeded the remaining funds. Instead of reducing the award to fit the funds, HUD skipped over the $7.5 million proposal and a $6.5 million proposal to fund five smaller projects near the same rank. The last award was adjusted slightly to reach the required total.

Aside from these variations, the process of awarding grants appears to have been a straightforward application of the ranking system among eligible applicants. All other things being equal, the use of the ranking scales should have increased the targeting of UDAGs within the pool of eligible cities. An application from a needy city could get 70 out of 100 possible points before the proposed project was even evaluated.

The criteria for eligibility were changed in 1987 with the addition of *labor surplus area*. After that time, cities had only to qualify on three out of seven criteria to become eligible. (Figure 5-1 describes all seven of the factors in use by 1987.)

During this time HUD supported the interpretation that UDAG funds were highly targeted. In its last annual report to Congress on the program (FY 1989), HUD stated that 84 percent of the money appropriated for FY 1988 and FY 1989 went to the one-third most impacted large cities. It also claimed that, over the life of the program, approximately two-thirds of the large city funds had been awarded to the one-third of the cities that were most impacted.

These various reports constitute a set of partial perspectives on UDAG's targeting performance. The early studies were conducted before the rating scale took effect and, in addition, they disagree with each other. The GAO looked at the effects of 1987 amendments on allocation rules and found that targeting, as measured by impaction, had declined somewhat in favor of a slight broadening of participation across region.[10] All of the studies focused on the large city program, leaving out the allocation of funds to small cities. Finally, variations in measures of need added confusion to the discussion. For example, Webman used the term "distress" to refer to the factors that HUD later called "impaction," while in its report to Congress HUD used only impaction to measure targeting, although its own formula used both impaction and distress. Obviously, one's judgment about targeting depends upon the measures used as well as one's standard for judging effectiveness.

MEASURING UDAG TARGETING

Clearly, there is no one "right" way to measure targeting, but all studies share the basic approach of relating some measure of program output to some measure of need. Most studies use one or both of the following measures of output: (1) the number of grants and (2) the total dollar amount awarded to cities. Dollars measure the allocational impact, but not the effects of HUD decision rules, except indirectly, because the amount of funds requested had little effect on the ranking of projects. The number of grants awarded to a city more clearly reflects the working of HUD decision rules but it is obviously affected by the number of applications from that city, a factor over which HUD had no control.

For the measures of need we use the HUD scales of impaction and distress, both separately and in combination. All of the previous research has used some combination of these measures or their individual elements. As explained in Chapter 4, HUD assigned each city a ranking on impaction and a ranking on distress. The scales were arranged so that a "1" meant the most deserving on that criterion (e.g., most impacted or most distressed). These rankings were used along with the merits of the proposal to evaluate applications.

The primary focus of our analysis will be upon the distribution of awards among the eligible cities. We must remember that the first instance of targeting came from the requirement that cities meet the eligibility threshold by showing need on three of the six, later seven, basic criteria. Our analysis of impaction and distress rankings deals with the distribution of grants among the pool of cities that cleared the eligibility threshold. This additional targeting is important because the first cut eliminated less than half of the nation's large cities from eligibility. Few observers would regard UDAG as highly targeted to the neediest cities, as envisioned by Secretary Harris, if the benefits were distributed among a majority of the nation's cities independently of need.

On the other hand, critics who wished to broaden the program probably did not worry, ultimately, about the stage at which targeting occurred. For them the bottom line was likely to be how their political unit had fared in the process. Hence, we report UDAG awards by region. We believe that region was an important variable because the regional caucuses of Congress became involved and much of the debate was cast in terms of regional distribution.

Most of the following analysis is based on the large cities program, as were all of the previously reported analyses. One obvious reason is simply that HUD has more data on large city applicants than on small ones. Yet this is an appropriate focus for other reasons as well. The intent of HUD, and especially of Secretary Harris in her presentation of the program to Congress in 1977, was to aid the large urban centers with their physical and economic problems. Over the life of the program from 1978 to 1989 large cities received 73 percent of the $4.6 billion appropriated by Congress. Nevertheless, we do include one comparison of large and small city distributions in the following analysis.

We examine total UDAG allocation decisions by various measures of need and by region and large versus small cities. Then we trace the relationship of UDAG grants to measures of need through time, seeking evidence of the dynamic political relationships hypothesized by Lowi.

Direct Effects of Eligibility Criteria and the Ranking System

Until 1983 the only deliberate targeting instrument in the system was the set of eligibility criteria. Initially, 333 cities were eligible. As a result of decisions made over the life of the program this number was expanded to 444. Yet even this larger pool represented only 52 percent of the nation's large cities and urban counties. The effect of this exclusion in terms of the opportunity to apply is quite clear. The effects on actual funding are much less clear because cities certainly did not submit applications at equal rates.

When the requested funds exceeded the amount available, HUD instituted its ranking system. What effect did this formula have within the pool of eligible applicants? Table 5-2 displays the detailed results of the first five decision rounds in which the ranking system had an effect. Here we see the same reductions in the number of applications that were funded as in Table 5-1. Whereas the prior approval rate had been 100 percent of eligible applications, it fell to 49 percent in June 1984. The low point was 25 percent in January 1985 and the high during this period was 60 percent in January 1986. Clearly, the formula had an effect, but did it increase the targeting of federal funds to needy cities?

We can get some measure of targeting from the impaction and distress rankings assigned to each application based upon the city from which it came. For example, in the June 1984 round the average impaction ranking of all applications was 169. The average impaction ranking of applications that were funded was 54. Since a lower ranking indicates more need, the formula resulted in a major increase in targeting, assuming one accepts impaction as a legitimate measure of need. We also see an improvement in the average distress ranking for that round, but the change is not as great as for impaction. This difference was probably due to the greater weight accorded to impaction in the formula used by HUD. The same pattern holds for the rest of the funding rounds during this time period. In each case there was a major focusing of resource allocations on the cities with the greatest need as measured by the impaction and distress scales, and in each case the change was greater on the impaction scale than on the distress scale.

So the ranking system had an effect, but the effect varied according to the measure of need. This result might not have been so important had the debate over appropriate measures been an academic exercise. It was not, for reasons we shall see in the next section.

Region and Need

In our political system the choice of need measures cannot be made in the abstract. Much of the impetus for the program had come from concern over the decaying large cities in what has become known as the rustbelt. Yet cities in other regions also had problems. Ideally, a targeting mechanism would seek out the most needy cities wherever they are. The

TABLE 5-2

Targeting on Impaction and Distress in Selected Funding Rounds

	Number of Grants			Average Impaction Rank		Average Distress Rank	
	Applications	Awards	%	All Applications	Awards	All Applications	Awards
June 84	84	41	48.8	169.0	54.3	160.0	92.2
Sept 84	151	69	45.7	173.1	59.6	159.4	93.8
Jan 85	142	36	25.4	157.6	43.9	147.5	78.1
May 85	138	81	58.7	132.0	63.8	131.4	89.3
Sept 85	74	40	54.1	150.9	67.2	132.3	112.5
Jan 86	91	55	60.4	149.2	75.5	121.6	91.0

Pockets of Poverty Omitted

political problem results from the facts that no single measure of need is clearly "right" in a substantive sense and all measures have geographical consequences. Since representation in Congress is geographically based, the political incentives are for members to support those measures that favor their home areas.

Table 5-3 demonstrates the regional and, therefore, political consequences of different choices. Here we have used impaction and distress scores from 1987, the time at which the greatest number of cities became eligible for UDAG funding. The "Most Impacted" and "Most Distressed" categories consist of the 148 neediest jurisdictions (one-third of the total) on each measure. In order to provide a consistent basis of comparison we have omitted applications that qualified under the "Pockets of Poverty Program." The regions are U.S. Census regions, which we have grouped into "rustbelt" and "non-rustbelt" because of the alignments in the congressional debates.

The table shows that the rustbelt has a higher percentage of neediest cities than other regions on either measure. But the differences are most pronounced for impaction. Nearly 56 percent of the rustbelt cities would be classified as neediest on the basis of impaction, while only 13 percent of the cities in the rest of the nation would be so classified. More important, the rustbelt has a full 80 percent of the nation's neediest cities according to this criterion.

The effects of different needs criteria can be most clearly seen in Table 5-4. Simply focusing the program on large cities would have given the rustbelt region, with 40 percent of the nation's population, 42 percent of the political units eligible for UDAGs, as compared with 58 percent for the non-rustbelt. Doing so would have been a distributive strategy with respect to region. The eligibility criteria improved the rustbelt's representation in the eligible pool slightly to 48 percent. The ranking of cities based upon distress alone would have given that region 55 percent of the cities classified as neediest and, therefore, most advantaged by the distribution formula. But a ranking based on impaction alone would have been most favorable to the rustbelt, giving it 80 percent of the cities in the most favored category. Of course, the formula was not based on one measure, but impaction carried the greatest weight in the formula.

Representatives of other regions spent a good bit of attention on the eligibility rule, *but even within the eligible pool the impaction score was targeting aid where the originators of the program had envisioned it going.* This point is demonstrated by Table 5-5, which shows the comparative success rates of applications from rustbelt and non-rustbelt regions. When the application process was competitive, defined here as those rounds in which not all applications were successful, the success rate among rustbelt applications was more than twice that of non-rustbelt applications.

TABLE 5-3

Number of Eligible Cities Meeting "Most Distressed" and "Most Impacted" Criteria, by Region

	Most Distressed		Most Impacted		
	Number	**%**	**Number**	**%**	**Total**
RUSTBELT REGIONS					
Northeast	2	4.8	32	76.2	42
Mid-Atlantic	29	40.8	55	77.5	71
East North Central	51	50.5	32	31.7	101
SUBTOTAL	82	38.3	119	55.6	214
NON-RUSTBELT					
West North Central	3	13.6	6	27.3	22
South Atlantic	10	17.5	9	15.8	57
East South Central	11	39.3	2	7.1	28
West South Central	13	33.3	1	2.6	39
Mountain	2	25.0	0	0.0	8
Pacific	15	24.6	3	4.9	61
Caribbean	12	92.3	8	61.5	13
SUBTOTAL	66	28.9	29	12.7	228
TOTAL	148	100.0	148	100.0	442*
RUSTBELT	82	55.4	119	80.4	
OTHER REGIONS	66	44.6	29	19.6	
TOTAL	148	100.0	148	100.0	442*

*Two of the total 444 cities referred to in the text were not included in this table because of missing data.

This fact may help to explain why the secretary chose to have fully funded rounds. Doing so could have been a means of spreading the wealth geographically and, therefore, of relieving political pressure on the program.

Large Cities and Small Cities

Table 5-6 examines the total allocations over the life of UDAG, including the small city program and the "pockets of poverty" allocations within the large city program. The bottom row shows that the total allocations clearly favored the rustbelt. With approximately 40 percent of the nation's population (by the 1980 Census), the rustbelt received 57 percent of UDAG funds.

Yet the regional impact varied markedly between the large cities program and the small cities program. Reading across the top row, we see that the rustbelt received 64 percent of the large city funds, almost two-thirds of the total. On the other hand, most of the small city funds (60.4%) went to the non-rustbelt regions.

Reading down we see that, while almost 73 percent of the total UDAG funds were distributed through the large city program, the relative dependence on the two programs varied by region. The rustbelt received 81 percent of its total UDAG funds through the large city program, but the non-rustbelt regions obtained only 61 percent of their funds in this manner.

The distributional impacts of the two UDAG programs are quite clear. Drawing inferences concerning the strategies or motives of various decision makers is always less clear. In earlier chapters we saw ample evidence that many representatives from non-rustbelt regions were unhappy with the allocation of grants. The evidence presented in this chapter shows that targeting on the basis of impaction in the large cities program had the effect of favoring the rustbelt. Since nearly three-fourths of the total UDAG dollars were distributed through this program, it is not surprising that others wanted a larger share.

On the other hand, the small cities program appears to have been leaning in the opposite direction. Actually, the percentage of distribution of small city funds between the two regions almost exactly matches their shares of the 1980 U.S. population. This is not to say that the program was untargeted, only that any targeting was unrelated to the regional lines of the large city program. Unfortunately, we do not have data on the approximately 10,000 eligible small cities to analyze targeting effects as we have done with the large cities. We can say that, with regard to the rustbelt/non-rustbelt division, the small cities program was distributive, rather than redistributive.

TABLE 5-4

Selection Criteria by Region

	Rustbelt	Non-Rustbelt	N
Large cities	42.0%	58.0%	849
Eligible cities	48.3%	51.7%	445
Most distressed	55.4%	44.6%	148
Most impacted	80.4%	19.6%	148

TABLE 5-5

Success Rates of Applications by Region

	Rustbelt		Non-Rustbelt	
	Submitted	Approved	Submitted	Approved
March 84	70	100.0%	57	100.0%
June 84	37	75.7%	47	27.7%
September 84	75	66.7%	76	25.0%
January 85	81	38.3%	61	8.2%
May 85	81	75.3%	57	35.1%
September 85	38	76.3%	36	30.6%
January 86	44	86.4%	47	36.2%
June 86	7	100.0%	27	100.0%
September 86	31	83.9%	19	26.3%
January 87	29	100.0%	27	100.0%
September 87	33	93.9%	24	91.7%
January 88	35	48.6%	23	15.0%
Pockets of Poverty Omitted				

TABLE 5-6

UDAG Dollars (in thousands) Distributed by City Size and Region

	Rustbelt	%	Non-Rustbelt	%	Total
Large Cities	$2,202,044	64.0	$1,238,164	36.0	$3,440,208
%	81.2		61.4		72.7
Small Cities	$510,963	39.6	$777,834	60.4	$1,288,797
%	18.8		38.6		27.3
					$4,729,005*

*Includes some funds that were recaptured in later years and allocated.

This finding confirms reports from UDAG staff that they viewed the small cities program as a distributive response to the political demands of the system. There may have been conscious decisions to make this program distributive in order to take some of the pressure off the redistributive large cities program, or the choice may have simply been the result of many political forces in a complex environment. But whether or not there was a conscious choice of a mixed strategy, the result was clearly mixed in the different allocation schemes that were used by the two programs.

UDAG THROUGH TIME

Our hypothesis, based on Lowi's work, regarding the pressure on redistributive programs, suggests that they will change over time or die. Thus far we have seen mixed evidence on HUD's response to its dilemma. The small cities program was distributive, but in the large cities program—the core of UDAG—the fortunes of non-rustbelt cities did not improve except in the occasional fully funded rounds. Now we will adopt a longer time frame for the large cities program, 1978–1989, to get the most complete perspective possible on HUD's actions. To do so we will use 1987 distress and impaction ratings for consistency because such data were not calculated before 1984. In addition, we will include the "pockets of poverty" that we excluded from some earlier analyses.

If HUD were responding to political pressure by broadening the large cities program, we would expect to find several things:

1. The average distress and impaction ratings of successful applications would increase over time because HUD would want to make the program more broad-based and inclusive.

2. The average dollar amount of the grants would decrease as HUD sought to distribute the money more widely.

3. The average size of cities receiving grants would decrease over time as HUD shifted funds away from the large cities that were the original targets of the program.

Table 5-7 shows that in each case these expectations were not fulfilled. The average impaction and distress ratings of successful applicants declined. The average city population of the successful applicant increased. Until 1989, at the very end of the program, the average grant size remained about the same despite declining funds. Thus, the widest view of the large cities program that we can take shows it continuing to target funds in the large cities program to impacted and distressed cities.

TABLE 5-7

**Average Need Scores, City Population, and Grant Size
of Successful Applications, 1978–1989**

Year	Impact	Distress	Population	Grant (× 1000)
1978	135	215	317,673	$3,624
1979	146	235	329,890	$3,385
1980	155	235	356,320	$4,874
1981	153	226	317,998	$2,868
1982	156	229	335,532	$3,294
1983	143	224	321,217	$3,792
1984	129	217	334,748	$3,032
1985	97	190	363,059	$3,264
1986	108	175	445,311	$3,603
1987	125	184	431,860	$3,381
1988	99	149	582,359	$4,134
1989	108	182	568,742	$1,943
Average	130	205	392,059	$3,432

CONCLUSION

Did UDAG remain a targeted program throughout its lifetime? The answer is mostly yes. The large cities program, where three-fourths of the money was, stayed highly targeted on need as measured by impaction and distress, especially the former. Here we see evidence of the program strategy. Targeting in this manner produced a very unequal distribution across regions, and this fact became the focal point of much criticism. Yet the small cities program, accounting for about one-fourth of the total allocations, clearly fits the distributive strategy with respect to region and may have been used to soften some of the criticism from non-rustbelt representatives.

HUD took other actions that appeared to make the entire program more distributive. Broadening the eligibility criteria certainly did increase the number of cities that could compete for grants. But as the eligibility criteria were relaxed, the ranking system took over and still directed funds predominantly to impacted and distressed cities, mainly in the rustbelt.

We cannot view HUD as a single actor in this matter. The work of the professional staff in the application of the criteria and the calculation of rankings clearly supported targeting. The secretary, however, found substantial discretion within the constraints of the annual budget by determining how far down the list to go in each funding round. By fully funding certain rounds he could reach specific targets with much lower scores than would normally be funded. In these rounds the non-rustbelt applications enjoyed equal success rates (100%) with the rustbelt applications.

The evidence in this chapter supports the conclusion of a mixed strategy, whether or not it was a conscious choice on anyone's part. HUD made a number of gestures toward a more distributive program, but the bulk of the funding remained highly targeted, possibly too highly targeted for its political survival. The remaining chapter summarizes the evidence and arguments from the entire volume regarding UDAG and the politics of redistribution.

NOTES

1. Randall B. Ripley and Grace A. Franklin, *Bureaucracy and Policy Implementation* (Homewood, Ill.: Dorsey Press, 1982), 198.

2. Ibid., 163–172.

3. P. David Sowell of the Department of Housing and Urban Development, interview by author, 15 August 1990, Washington, D.C.

4. Graham T. Allison, *Essence of Decision: Explaining the Cuban Missile Crisis* (Boston, Mass.: Little, Brown, 1971).

5. Robert S. Montjoy and Laurence J. O'Toole, "Toward a Theory of Policy Implementation: An Organizational Perspective," *Public Administration Review* 38-5 (September/October 1979): 465–476.

6. Yong Hyo Cho and David Puryear, "Distressed Cities: Targeting HUD Programs," in *Urban Revitalization*, ed. Donald B. Rosenthal (Beverly Hills: Sage Publications, 1980), 199–200. Cho and Puryear, 209.

7. John R. Gist and R. Carter Hill, "The Economics of Choice in the Allocation of Federal Grants: An Empirical Test," *Public Choice* 36-1: 72.

8. Jerry A. Webman, "UDAG: Targeting Economic Development," *Political Science Quarterly* 96-2 (Summer 1981): 202.

9. For insight into how Secretary Pierce and his subordinates manipulated the funding list to fund favored projects, see the testimony of former HUD Deputy Assistant Secretary for Program Policy Development and Evaluation Dubois L. Gilliam in Congress, House, Committee on Government Operations, *Abuses, Favoritism, and Mismanagement in HUD Programs (Part 5)*, 101st Cong., 2nd Sess., 30 April 1990, 75–89.

10. General Accounting Office, *Urban Development Action Grants—Effects of the 1987 Amendments on Project Selection* (Washington, D.C.: U.S. General Accounting Office, 1989), 13.

6

The Politics of Redistributing Urban Aid: Issues, Findings, and Conclusions

This book explores the politics of redistributing urban aid by conducting an in-depth case study of the Urban Development Action Grant (UDAG) program. It develops and tests the thesis that large redistributive programs such as UDAG automatically generate political opposition powerful enough to transform them into distributive programs or to lead to their termination. A corollary is that even very substantial bureaucratic discretion will not enable administrators of such programs to stop the effects described.

The thesis merits examination for both practical and theoretical reasons. Its practical implications relate to current interest in a renewed targeting of urban aid to particularly needy cities. Simply put, programs of this type will survive only so long as substantial numbers of nonbeneficiaries are motivated and willing to pay. Such programs will thus involve investments of political capital, as well as fiscal and bureaucratic capital.

The theoretical component of the analysis draws on the concept of policy types to help explain why redistributive programs such as UDAG are difficult to keep on course. The UDAG program and the policy it embodied were redistributive. Policies of this type involve the channeling of resources to a limited class of eligible recipients, and therefore involve some degree of sacrifice on the part of the much larger class of nonrecipients. Targeting, as examined here, is the process of determining the class of beneficiaries that can receive support from a redistributive program. It involves defining and implementing criteria for project eligibility and selection.

In the work of Theodore Lowi, discussed in Chapter 2 of this book, redistributive policies are contrasted with policies that are distributive. A classic example of the distributive policy here is the river and harbors project grants program. As Lowi puts it, distributive policies function "almost on a basis of come one, come all." The class of potential recipients is virtually unlimited, so that there is no clearly definable group that comprehend themselves as taxed to support others without themselves benefitting. Thus there are powerful *political* differences between redistributive and distributive policies.

Chapter 2 develops the rationale for expecting the emergence of pressures to transform redistributive programs into distributive ones. The argument is that if a congressionally mandated federal urban aid program is in fact targeted, then over time the allocation decisions will displease a large number of individual members in their capacities as district representatives. If the impetus that stimulated the original passage wanes, as is often the case, then the program may be left without support in budgetary battles. The needed support can be gained by broadening the targeted pool of beneficiaries, thus making the program more distributive. Indeed, evidence in support of this rationale can be seen in the experience of several major redistributive programs prior to UDAG, including the War on Poverty, the Economic Development Administration, and the Comprehensive Employment and Training Act.

Program managers charged with achieving targeting objectives are surely aware of this dilemma. The sizeable discretion they have in their administrative capacity allows them to make choices. They can remain true to their mandate and risk loss of support. Or, they can seek to broaden support by distributing benefits more widely, thus undermining the targeting intent of the original mandate. A third possibility is to send mixed signals, at times appearing to satisfy demands for broader distribution, and at times appearing to satisfy the original redistributive mandate.

This line of argument, as developed in Chapter 2, leads to two main questions that carry the analysis in the remaining chapters. First is whether, as expected, there arose during UDAG's lifetime external pressures to broaden the allocation of benefits. The second question has to do with the behaviors exhibited by program administrators. The premise underlying these two questions is that this type of program automatically generates political forces that lead to its transformation or demise.

Chapter 3 reviews the history of the UDAG program. The UDAG bill recommended by the Carter administration in 1977 clearly intended precise targeting of support to those of America's cities that were facing the greatest "physical decline and economic deterioration," in effect the large cities of the rustbelt. Nevertheless, numerous measures directly or indirectly broadened the pool of potential beneficiaries during the life of the program.

- Twenty-five percent of the funding was set aside for small cities, many of which had little in common with the large cities that were UDAG's originally intended beneficiaries.

- Urban counties were added to the program, even though many of them contained the suburbs that urban observers claimed contributed to the problems of large cities.

- Furthermore, cities that were not otherwise eligible were given permission to apply for grants if they had pockets of poverty that qualified. This provision added more than 200 cities to the list of eligible candidates for UDAG funding.

- HUD designed its eligibility criteria so that over 50 percent of the nation's large cities and over 10,000 small cities qualified as "severely distressed." This strategy had the effect of broadening the targeting of UDAG substantially beyond the range envisioned by HUD Secretary Patricia Roberts Harris in early 1977.

- Requirements for citizen participation plans and housing assistance plans were dropped. The result was to reduce the paperwork needed for applications, thus making it easier for more communities, especially small ones, to compete for funding.

- The addition of labor surplus area as a criterion under which cities could qualify for funding had the effect of increasing the number of eligible cities.

- Without giving an explanation for why it did so, HUD reduced the threshold requirement for qualifying under the pre-1940 housing criterion from 33.98 percent to 21 percent. This criterion had created much controversy because it so clearly favored the older cities of the rustbelt region.

- When congressional delegations from sunbelt cities threatened to withdraw support for UDAG, a two-pot system was implemented that allowed those cities to receive more funding.

Chapter 4 reviews five major government studies of UDAG conducted during the life of the program. The nature of the issues these studies addressed, as well as the findings they reached, lend support to the main thesis of this book. The studies, one of which was performed by HUD and four of which were performed by the General Accounting Office (GAO) at the request of Congress, addressed three major and recurring issues or problems in the targeting of intergovernmental aid: the criteria for eligibility, the formula for selection, and the degree of participation by eligible cities.

The simple fact that these major studies all addressed issues directly related to targeting provides powerful circumstantial evidence that members of Congress were paying close attention to the distributional effects of the UDAG program. The findings of the studies indicate the complex and difficult nature of targeting in UDAG.

A major problem with eligibility rules was the difficulty of identifying criteria that were unambiguously valid and reliable indicators of urban distress. A complicating aspect of the selection criteria, discussed in both Chapters 4 and 5, is that no selection rules could have been politically neutral. HUD's choices would have generated opposition no matter whether they favored the targeting goals of the UDAG program itself, or favored economic development goals regardless of need. Since much economic development activity was taking place in the sunbelt, a reliance on selection criteria that emphasized development regardless of need would have tended to shift resources away from the rustbelt. With regard to participation, the dependence of the UDAG program on the initiative and ability of local governments to complete the application process necessarily limited the precision with which the granting agency could target program resources.

The sequence in which these issues came into play in the government studies also suggests that distributive pressures were indeed at work as expected. Relatively early in the program the issue of eligibility fairness was of concern to some members of Congress because their cities were not eligible under the HUD formula. After the selection system was instituted, congressional concerns turned to fairness on this score and also to the problem of participation. Also, as indicated in both Chapters 4 and 5, HUD's reactions to some of the GAO studies suggest the complex politics of targeting in the UDAG program. In particular, HUD's report to Congress that the percentage of funds going to most needy cities increased after 1987, contradicting a GAO report that found UDAG funds were being spread more widely, suggests the ambiguity and the political volatility of the targeting problem.

Chapter 5 explores who got what in the complex political arena of UDAG. Analysis of grant awards over the life of the program indicates that despite the political concerns and pressures for greater distributiveness, the large cities portion of UDAG, where three-fourths of the money was, stayed highly targeted on need as measured by impaction and distress, especially the former. This finding represents evidence of what we have termed the program strategy: HUD administrators exercised discretion in ways that led to the kind of redistributive outcomes that the UDAG policy had intended. Targeting in this manner produced a very unequal distribution across regions, and this result in turn led to criticism. The small cities program, accounting for about one-fourth of the total allocations, fit what we have called the distributive strategy: it allocated funding in proportion to the population (of the rustbelt and non-rustbelt regions).

In sum, several types of data and analyses support a fairly consistent interpretation of the life and death of UDAG. Conceived as a targeted, redistributive program, it was predictably subjected to political pressures in the direction of becoming more distributive. HUD administrators exercised their very considerable discretion in ways consistent with the interpretation that they followed a mixed strategy in responding to the tension between their original mandate and increasing distributive pressures. Program rules were revised to allow broadened access to funding; the large cities program remained targeted to need; the small cities program was essentially distributive; HUD's interpretations of targeting success were at times ambiguous in relation to the data.

The tale of UDAG can be read as cautionary in both practical and theoretical terms. Those who would design and implement highly targeted urban aid programs can expect a surge of distributive pressures to develop over time. The conceptual framework of policy types supports a theory-based explanation of why these pressures arise and of the automaticity with which they do so.* Reliance on short-term programs may be one way of responding. Additional steps might include building targeting objectives very explicitly into the original legislation and designing fairly simple application procedures. Given the evident complexity of targeting in programs of this type, however, the implications of the UDAG experience for a future effort would need to be assessed in relation to the specific details of policy design and implementation.

---

*The naturalness and inevitability with which distributive pressures rise to meet redistributive policies, as explored using the concept of policy types, suggests an analogy in the political arena to Charles Lindblom's characterization of "the market as prison." In both cases, an institutional arena automatically gives rise to forces that constrain policy outcomes. In this interpretation, the automatic nature of the response, which Lindblom ascribes to the nature of *market* incentives, is seen also in the *polity* as institutionalized in the constitutional framework for democratic government in the United States. See Charles E. Lindblom, "The Market as Prison," *Journal of Politics* 44-2 (May 1982): 324–336.

Selected Bibliography

Allison, Graham T. *Essence of Decision: Explaining the Cuban Missile Crisis*. Boston, Mass.: Little, Brown, 1971.

Babbie, Earl R. *The Practice of Social Research*. Belmont, Calif.: Wadsworth, 1986.

Bandow, Doug. "Corporate America: Uncle Sam's Favorite Welfare Client." *Business and Society Review* 55 (Fall 1985): 48–54.

Banfield, Edward C. *The Unheavenly City Revisited*. Boston: Little, Brown, 1974.

Bickman, Leonard, ed. *Using Program Theory in Education*. San Francisco: Jossey-Bass, 1987.

Bogart, William T., and Jon Erickson. "On the Design of Equalizing Grants." *Publius* 19 (Spring 1989): 33–46.

Bollens, John C., and Henry J. Schmandt. *The Metropolis*. New York: Harper & Row, 1965.

Cho, Yong Hyo, and David Puryear. "Distressed Cities: Targeting HUD Programs." In *Urban Revitalization*, ed. Donald B. Rosenthal, 191–210. Beverly Hills: Sage Publications, 1980.

Copeland, Gary W., and Kenneth J. Meier. "Pass the Biscuits, Pappy: Congressional Decision Making and Federal Grants." *American Politics Quarterly* 12 (January 1984): 3–21.

Cyert, Richard M., and James G. March. *A Behavioral Theory of the Firm*. Englewood Cliffs, N.J.: Prentice-Hall, 1963.

Dilger, Robert Jay. *The Sunbelt/Snowbelt Controversy: The War over Federal Funds*. New York: New York University Press, 1982.

Dye, Thomas R. "Targeting Intergovernmental Aid." *Social Science Quarterly* 68 (September 1987): 443–446.

———. *American Federalism: Competition Among Governments.* Lexington, Mass.: Lexington Books, 1990.

Dye, Thomas R., and Thomas L. Hurley. "The Responsiveness of Federal and State Grants to Urban Problems." *Journal of Politics* 40 (February 1978): 196–207.

Farr, Cheryl. "Encouraging Local Economic Development: The State of the Practice." In *1990 Municipal Yearbook,* 15–29. Washington, D.C.: International City Management Association, 1990.

Fossett, James W. *Federal Aid to Big Cities: The Politics of Dependence.* Washington, D.C.: Brookings Institution, 1983.

Gatons, Paul K., and Michael Brintnall. "Competitive Grants: The UDAG Approach." In *Urban Economic Development,* eds. Richard D. Bingham and John P. Blair, 115–137. Beverly Hills: Sage Publications, 1984.

Gist, John R. "Urban Development Action Grants: Design and Implementation." In *Urban Revitalization,* ed. Donald B. Rosenthal, 237–252. Beverly Hills: Sage Publications, 1980.

Gist, John R., and R. Carter Hill. "The Economics of Choice in the Allocation of Federal Grants: An Empirical Test." *Public Choice* 36-1 (1981): 63–73.

Greider, William. *The Education of David Stockman and Other Americans.* New York: E. P. Dutton, 1982.

Hansen, Susan B. "Targeting in Economic Development: Comparative State Perspectives." *Publius* 19 (Spring 1989): 47–62.

Hayes, Michael T. *Lobbyists and Legislators.* New Brunswick, N.J.: Rutgers University Press, 1981.

Heilman, John G., and Douglas J. Watson. "Publicization, Privatization, Synthesis, Tradition: Options for Public-Private Configuration." *International Journal of Public Administration* 16-1 (January 1993): 107–137.

Jacobs, Susan S., and Elizabeth A. Roistacher. "The Urban Impacts of HUD's Urban Development Action Grant Program, or, Where's the Action in Action Grants?" In *The Urban Impacts of Federal Policies,* ed. Norman J. Glickman, 335–362. Baltimore: Johns Hopkins University Press, 1980.

Johnson, Kirk. "Take Our Poor, Angry Hartford Tells Suburbs." *New York Times,* 11 February 1991, A1 and A13.

Kellow, Aynsley. "Promoting Elegance in Policy Theory: Simplifying Lowi's Arenas of Power." *Policy Studies Journal* 16-4 (Summer 1988): 713–724.

Lindblom, Charles E. "The Market as Prison." *Journal of Politics* 44-2 (May 1982): 324–336.

Lineberry, Robert L. *American Public Policy: What Government Does and What Difference It Makes.* New York: Harper & Row, 1978.

Lowi, Theodore J. "American Business, Public Policy, Case-Studies, and Political Theory." *World Politics* XVI-4 (July 1964): 677–715.

———. "Decision Making vs. Policy Making: Toward an Antidote for Technocracy." *Public Administration Review* 30-3 (May–June 1970): 314–325.

———. "Four Systems of Policy, Politics, and Choice." *Public Administration Review* 32-4 (July–August 1972): 298–310.

Mauro, Frank J., and Glenn Yago. "State Government Targeting in Economic Development: The New York Experience." *Publius* 19 (Spring 1989): 63–82.

Montjoy, Robert S., and Laurence J. O'Toole, Jr. "Toward a Theory of Policy Implementation: An Organizational Perspective." *Public Administration Review* 38-5 (September/October 1979): 465–476.

———. "Policy Instruments and Politics: Multiple Regression and Intergovernmental Aid." *State and Local Government Review* 23-2 (Spring 1991): 51–59.

Moore, Paul D. "General Purpose Aid in New York State: Targeting Issues and Measures." *Publius* 19 (Spring 1989): 17–31.

Morgan, David R. and Mei-Chiang Shih. "Targeting State and Federal Aid to City Needs." *State and Local Government Review* 23-2 (Spring 1991): 60–68.

Nathan, Richard P. "The Politics of Printouts." In *The Politics of Numbers,* eds. William Alonso and Paul Starr, 331–342. New York: Russell Sage, 1987.

Patton, Michael Q. *Utilization-Focused Evaluation,* 2nd ed. Beverly Hills: Sage Publications, 1986.

Pelissero, John P. "State Aid and City Needs: An Examination of Residual State Aid to Large Cities." *Journal of Politics* 46 (August 1984): 916–935.

———. "Welfare and Education Aid to Cities." *Social Science Quarterly* 66 (June 1985): 444–452.

Peterson, Lorna. "The Demise of the Urban Development Action Grant Program: A Bibliography." Monticello, Ill.: Vance Bibliographies, undated.

President's Commission on Privatization. *Privatization: Toward More Effective Government.* Washington, D.C.: U.S. Government Printing Office, 1988.

Reed, Ingrid W. "Life and Death of UDAG: An Assessment Based on Eight Projects in Five New Jersey Cities." *Publius* 19 (Summer 1989): 93–109.

Rich, Michael J. "Hitting the Target: The Distributional Impacts of the Urban Development Action Grant Program." *Urban Affairs Quarterly* 17-3 (March 1982): 285–301.

————. "Distributive Politics and the Allocation of Federal Grants." *American Political Science Review* 83-1 (March 1989): 193–213.

Rieselbach, Leroy N. "Congress and Policy Change: Issues, Answers, and Prospects." In *Congress and Policy Change*, eds. Gerald C. Wright, Jr., Leroy N. Rieselbach, and Lawrence C. Dodd, 257–289. New York: Agathon Press, 1986.

Ripley, Randall B., and Grace A. Franklin. *Bureaucracy and Policy Implementation*. Homewood, Ill.: Dorsey Press, 1982.

————. *Congress, the Bureaucracy, and Public Policy*, 4th ed. Chicago: Dorsey Press, 1987.

Saltzstein, Alan. "Federal Categorical Aid to Cities: Who Needs It Versus Who Wants It. "*Western Political Quarterly* 30 (September 1977): 377–383.

Shepsle, Kenneth A., and Barry R. Weingast. "Political Preference for the Pork Barrel: A Generalization." *American Journal of Political Science* 25 (February 1981): 96–111.

Stein, Robert M. "The Allocation of State Aid to Local Governments: An Examination of Interstate Variations." In *State and Local Roles in the Federal System*, Advisory Commission on Intergovernmental Relations, 203. Washington, D.C.: U.S. Government Printing Office, 1982.

Stein, Robert M., and Keith E. Hamm. "A Comparative Analysis of Targeting Capacity of State and Federal Intergovernmental Aid Allocations: 1977, 1982." *Social Science Quarterly* 68 (September 1987): 447–465.

Stockman, David A. *The Triumph of Politics*. New York: Harper & Row, 1986.

The Institute for Professional and Executive Development, Inc. *UDAG Update*. Washington, D.C.: Institute for Professional and Executive Development, 1984.

U.S. Congress. House. Committee on Banking, Finance, and Urban Affairs. *Housing and Community Development Act of 1977*. 95th Cong., 1st Sess., 24 February 1977.

————. Committee on Banking, Finance, and Urban Affairs. *Housing and Community Development Act of 1977*. 95th Cong., 1st Sess., 28 February 1977.

————. Committee on Banking, Finance, and Urban Affairs. *Housing and Community Development Act of 1977*. 95th Cong., 1st Sess., 1 March 1977.

————. Committee on Banking, Finance, and Urban Affairs. *Housing and Community Development Act of 1977*. 95th Cong., 1st Sess., 9 March 1977.

————. Committee on Banking, Finance, and Urban Affairs. *Compilation of the Housing and Community Development Act of 1977*. 95th Cong., 1st Sess., October 1977.

———. Committee on Governmental Operations. *Abuses, Favoritism, and Mismanagement in HUD Programs (Part 5)*. 101st Cong., 2nd Sess., 30 April 1990.

U.S. Congress. Senate. Committee on Banking, Housing, and Urban Affairs. *Housing, Community Development, and Mass Transportation Authorizations—1986: Hearing before the Subcommittee on Housing and Urban Affairs*. 99th Cong., 1st Sess., 15 April 1985.

U.S. Department of Housing and Urban Development. "Community Development Block Grants; Clarification and Changes to Urban Development Action Grant Rules." *Federal Register* 45-93 (12 May 1980): 31,262.

———. Office of Community Planning and Development. *Urban Development Action Grant Program—Second Annual Report*. Washington, D.C.: U.S. Department of Housing and Urban Development, 1980.

———. Office of the Assistant Secretary for Community Planning and Development. "Community Development Block Grants; Urban Development Action Grants; Final Rule." *Federal Register* 47-36 (23 February 1982): 7982–7995.

———. Office of Policy Development and Research. *An Impact Evaluation of the Urban Development Action Grant Program*. Washington, D.C.: U.S. Department of Housing and Urban Development, 1982.

———. Office of Community Planning and Development. *1982 Consolidated Annual Report to Congress on Community Development Progress*. Washington, D.C.: U.S. Department of Housing and Urban Development, 1982.

———. Office of the Assistant Secretary for Community Planning and Development. "Urban Development Action Grants Distress Criteria." *Federal Register* 49-17 (25 January 1984): 3074–3076.

———. Office of the Assistant Secretary for Community Planning and Development. *1984 Consolidated Annual Report to Congress and Community Development Programs*. Washington, D.C.: U.S. Department of Housing and Urban Development, 1984.

———. Office of Community Planning and Development. *1985 Consolidated Annual Report to Congress and Community Development Programs*. Washington D.C.: U.S. Department of Housing and Urban Development, 1985.

———. Office of Community Planning and Development. *1986 Consolidated Annual Report to Congress on Community Development Programs*. Washington, D.C.: U.S. Department of Housing and Urban Development, 1986.

———. Office of Community Planning and Development. *1987 Consolidated Annual Report to Congress and Community Development Programs*. Washington, D.C.: U.S. Department of Housing and Urban Development, 1987.

————. Office of Community Planning and Development. *1988 Consolidated Annual Report to Congress on Community Development Programs.* Washington D.C.: U.S. Department of Housing and Urban Development, 1988.

————. Office of Community Planning and Development. *Report to Congress on Community Development Programs—1989.* Washington, D.C.: U.S. Department of Housing and Urban Development, 1989.

————. Office of the Assistant Secretary for Public Affairs. *New Directions in Housing and Urban Policy: 1981–1989.* Washington, D.C.: U.S. Department of Housing and Urban Development, 1989.

————. Office of Community Planning and Development. *Annual Report to Congress on the Urban Development Action Grant Program—FY 1989.* Washington, D.C.: U.S. Department of Housing and Urban Development, 1990.

————. *Analysis of the Income Cities Earn from UDAG Projects,* by David Rymph and Jack Underhill. Washington, D.C.: U.S. Department of Housing and Urban Development, 1990.

U.S. General Accounting Office. *Criteria for Participation in the Urban Development Action Grant Program Should Be Refined.* Washington, D.C.: U.S. General Accounting Office, 1980.

————. *HUD Review of Urban Development Action Grant to Wilmington, N.C.* Washington, D.C.: U.S. General Accounting Office, 1986.

————. *Insights into Major Urban Development Action Grant Issues.* Washington, D.C.: U.S. General Accounting Office, 1984.

————. *The Urban Development Action Grant Application Selection System: Basis, Criticisms, and Alternatives.* Washington, D.C.: U.S. General Accounting Office, 1985.

————. *Urban Development Action Grants—Effects of the 1987 Amendments on Project Selection.* Washington D.C.: U.S. General Accounting Office, 1989.

Vogler, David J. *The Politics of Congress,* 4th ed. Boston: Allyn & Bacon, 1983.

Ward, Peter D. "The Measurement of Federal and State Responsiveness to Urban Problems." *Journal of Politics* 43 (February 1981): 83–99.

Webman, Jerry A. "UDAG: Targeting Urban Economic Development." *Political Science Quarterly* 96-2 (Summer 1981): 189–207.

Index

About the Authors

DOUGLAS J. WATSON holds the degree of Doctor of Philosophy from Auburn University. He has served as city manager of Auburn, Alabama, since 1982 and has received numerous awards for his work as a public administrator. A native of Rochester, New York, he grew up in Scranton, Pennsylvania.

JOHN G. HEILMAN holds a Ph.D. from New York University and has served on the faculty at Auburn University since 1973. Presently, he is Associate Dean of the College of Liberal Arts and Professor of Political Science. He is a native of New York City.

ROBERT S. MONTJOY holds a Ph.D. from Indiana University. Prior to joining the Auburn University faculty in 1979 he taught at the University of Virginia, where he gained first-hand experience with targeting issues while designing an aid distribution formula for the Commonwealth of Virginia. He now directs the Master of Public Administration program at Auburn.